PETERSFIELD
AT WAR

DAVID JEFFERY

T0333143

The History Press

Title page picture: Royal Tank Corps on manoeuvres near Petersfield in 1938. (*Imperial War Museum*)

First published in 2004 by Sutton Publishing Limited

Reprinted in 2009 by
The History Press
The Mill, Brimscombe Port
Stroud, Gloucestershire, GL5 2QG
www.thehistorypress.co.uk

British Library Cataloguing in Publication Data.
A catalogue record for this book is available from the British Library.

ISBN 978 0 7509 3672 9

Typesetting and origination by Sutton Publishing Limited
Printed in Malta

Contents

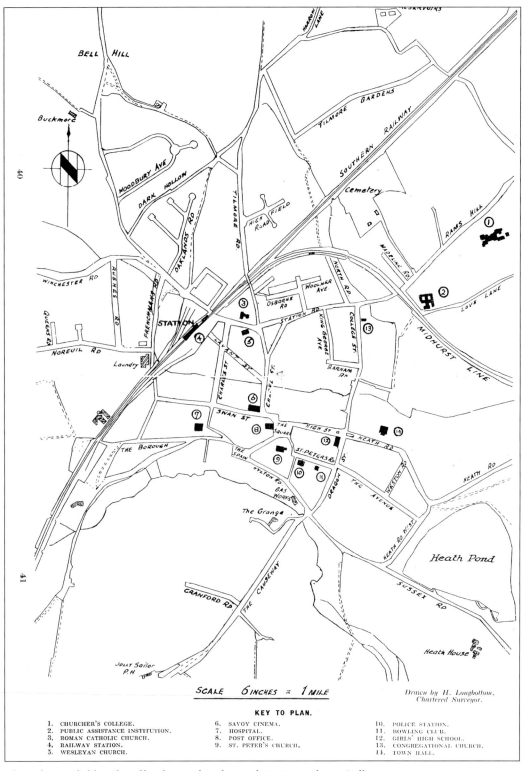

Plan of Petersfield in the official town brochure of 1938. (Author's Collection)

SCALE   6 INCHES = 1 MILE

Drawn by H. Longbottom,
Chartered Surveyor.

KEY TO PLAN.

1. CHURCHER'S COLLEGE.
2. PUBLIC ASSISTANCE INSTITUTION.
3. ROMAN CATHOLIC CHURCH.
4. RAILWAY STATION.
5. WESLEYAN CHURCH.
6. SAVOY CINEMA.
7. HOSPITAL.
8. POST OFFICE.
9. ST. PETER'S CHURCH.
10. POLICE STATION.
11. BOWLING CLUB.
12. GIRLS' HIGH SCHOOL.
13. CONGREGATIONAL CHURCH.
14. TOWN HALL.

Foreword & Acknowledgements

At first glance, the title of this book appears to be a misnomer – Petersfield hardly experienced any enemy action and certainly none of the horrors which afflicted so many larger communities during the Second World War. But this is not intended as a history book, the military events having been amply documented in other works: it is rather a snapshot of a community living through six years of a war to all intents and purposes happening elsewhere; one which attempts to provide a social chronicle of Petersfield through the eyes of its contemporary residents whose lives were certainly coloured, and possibly impeded or enhanced, by the events of 1939–45. To this end, I have devoted a roughly equal amount of space to the recollections of the individuals who found themselves in the locality as to the purely factual account of events.

Oral history is a precious commodity. However, it does bring its own problems: it is like a flawed diamond whose individual facets only partly reflect reality yet contain sufficient truth and light to be accepted as a gem nevertheless. Carlyle called history 'a distillation of rumour', but I would hope that my account – or rather the accounts of my sympathetic and generous contributors – stood for more than that. As a Londoner born and bred, I trust that I have maintained a certain objectivity (despite, at the same time, being enamoured of the town); selection, after all, is inevitable, but I have preferred the anecdotal over the apocryphal, the complimentary over the conflictual.

Any process of selection is simultaneously one of rejection, so I apologise in advance for any inadvertent omissions, errors, or misjudgements which may offend those more familiar with the details than I am. In exploring and exploiting the *Hants and Sussex News*, I have eschewed private details occurring under the rubric 'Petersfield Petty Sessions', likewise personal tragedies reported under 'News from our Men', where it would have been quite invidious to find that I had omitted even one person among all those who fought – and died – so courageously during the war. For the purposes of the book, I spoke to around seventy people and received invaluable information from several others, but perhaps equally poignant were the personal mementoes, family albums, private photographs and other memorabilia which everyone has been gracious and generous enough to show me. For this, I thank my contributors most sincerely; my only hope is that this book does them and their memories justice. Their stories, after all, are our history.

In the process of writing the book, I became aware that I was describing not only the events of the war period, but also the changes which Petersfield itself and its inhabitants were living through, from the 'old Petersfield' of the 1930s to the newly emerging town of the 1950s. In fact, these three decades saw relatively small changes compared with the rapid, sometimes unforgivable, changes of the 1960s. From our new standpoint on the cusp of the twenty-first century, therefore, our three decades are most emphatically the 'old' Petersfield, and these insights seem tantalisingly close to the older generations.

I have deliberately left ladies' names in their married form where appropriate, so that they may be more easily identified by the reader; their maiden names appear in the short biographical section at the back of the book.

As well as the individual thanks I owe to everyone I have interviewed, I would like to acknowledge especially the help I have received in compiling this volume from Doreen Binks and Mary Ray of the Petersfield Museum, Gillian and Vaughan Clarke of *Sheet News*, Tony Cross and the Hampshire County Council Museums Service for permission to reproduce prints by Flora Twort, Chris Lloyd for his collection of insignia and memorabilia, Simon Fletcher of Sutton Publishing, David Lee of Wessex Film and Sound Archive for the loan of recording equipment, John Sadden of Petersfield Library, and, for the bulk of the photographs which appear in these pages, Petersfield Museum archives.

Finally, I thank my daughter Anna-Louise for reading the manuscript and for making many helpful suggestions.

David Jeffery

Introduction:
Petersfield in the 1930s

How to characterise a decade? Nonagenarian and octogenarian Petersfielders have amply provided a picture of the era: the predominantly agricultural community, the nascent social and cultural life of the town, the everyday atmosphere and the unusual happenings.

Joan Bullen and John Bridle both remember the 1920s and 1930s with equal lucidity, a time when they could claim to know everyone they saw in Petersfield. John and some friends would enjoy rambling over to Butser and then arrange a dance in Winton House in the evening; Joan and John both lived in Hylton Road and could look out of their bedroom windows across the fields where a herd of cows would be grazing and, beyond, towards the Weston hopfields and Butser; John and his wife-to-be enjoyed their favourite walk across Buckmore Farm's wild-flower laden meadows; Joan also remembers hiking and country dancing and the Bedales' Shakespeare plays which were put on every Christmas. It was a time when Petersfield had at least two dairies and two farriers; the 'Electric' cinema (with Mrs LeGoubin playing the piano at the front); electric lighting, which had only relatively recently been installed in the streets; and when the British Legion gave tea parties for children.

But this rural idyll did have another, more irksome and seemingly less prosperous, side: Amy Freeman talks of the impecunious existence of many hard-working people; of the total lack of holidays for the (often large) families; of the need for children to leave school at fourteen and start work to help increase family incomes; of the harsh regimes in schools for even the youngest children.

The churches played an important social, as well as religious, role in people's lives. Families might go to church three times on a Sunday and Sunday school outings were a rare but welcome treat; besides St Peter's and St Laurence's, the so-called 'free churches' prospered: the Congregational (now United Reformed) church, the (Wesleyan) Methodist church in Station Road, and the 'Primitive Methodists' in Windsor Road, drew large congregations. In fact, it was in the 1930s that the two types of Methodism began preliminary discussions which eventually brought them together in March 1942. Mr Fuller, the Lavant Street grocer, was described as 'a pillar of the Congregational chapel'. The first meetings of local Quakers took place at Bedales Lodge at Steep in 1934 and an Elim church was also started in the Corn Exchange building by Mr Victor Walker in the 1930s. There were also the Plymouth Brethren who met at 60 Station Road. Finally, the Salvation Army, active in Petersfield since the end of the nineteenth century, had its own hall in Swan Street and used to conduct open-air services in The Square and on the

The corner of The Avenue and Dragon Street in the 1930s. (Petersfield Museum)

Heath; it also attended the Taro Fair and participated in marches through the town in the 1930s.

For boys, the Wolf Cubs and Boy Scouts groups, among the first in the country to be set up after the foundation of the Scouting Movement in 1908, provided activities, outings and excitement and there were dedicated leaders such as Charles Dickins, the High Street dentist, who spent many years organising displays, camps, and participation in Scout jamborees.

Petersfield Carnival Week took place annually in June at the Carnival Park, situated opposite the Jolly Sailor. It lasted for a week, starting with the crowning of a Carnival Queen, continuing with displays, dances and concerts, a huge fancy-dress procession, athletic events and a boxing tournament, and finishing with a lantern and torchlight parade to the grand evening concert in the Drill Hall. Proceeds went to Petersfield Hospital, a fund for a new Town Hall and to local organisations.

In many ways, the farming community dominated Petersfield in the 1930s. First, small farms proliferated in and around the town, most of which have now disappeared completely: Herne, Buckmore, Lord's, Tilmore, Broadway, Penns, Weston, to name but those which were situated closest to the centre of the town.

Fuller's grocery shop, Lavant Street, in the 1930s. (Petersfield Museum)

Some of the same names still exist, of course, but they are now associated with a housing estate and a school, an estate for park homes, or District Council offices! Secondly, the Wednesday cattle markets brought a whole population of farmers, drovers, buyers, stockmen and breeders to the very heart of Petersfield, where their presence was keenly felt (and appreciated) by the residents. It could easily be argued that they contributed in no small way to Petersfield's sense of community. Thirdly, Petersfielders depended to a large extent on the products of farming: there was the abattoir next to the Grange and several minor slaughterhouses adjacent to the towns' butchers, all of which provided specialised employment; meat, milk and poultry products were brought fresh into the town to their numerous retail outlets which everyone benefited from. In short, agricultural wealth generated general wealth. Fourthly, every ordinary citizen well understood and appreciated the contribution that farmers made to their existence, even if that merely meant the provision of a regular pint or two of milk from a churn at the local farm.

Fifthly, much of Petersfield's historically indigenous professional expertise lay in the work of its agricultural workers who, together with the specialist carters, sheep-dippers and shearers, farriers, thatchers, pig rearers, charcoal-burners, hop-pickers and tellers, and horse workers, constituted a breadth of know-how probably unrivalled in the South Downs. Many schoolboys and girls assisted the regular farmworkers at certain times of the year, particularly at harvest-time, and so absorbed a considerable amount of knowledge about farming – and earned them-selves a little pocket money in the process.

It was during the thirties, however, that farming methods and practices began to change radically. Most farmers used horse power until the beginning of the war, when the first (Fordson) tractors came in, some on lease-lend from America. In 1933, farmers became hostile towards the petty margins being earned from milk production locally and it was in that year that the Milk Marketing Board was formed. Peter Winscom's cows were being hand-milked until 1937, and he would transport the filled churns by horse and cart to the South Eastern Farmers dairy by the station (now Dairy Crest), where the milk was processed.

Electricity, and therefore electric milking machines, came in during the war period. Water used to come from the farm well until a domestic supply was installed in the early war years. John Lovell helped with the threshing at Bolinge Hill Farm during the war and they used a wind engine to lift water – one of the few such engines in the area.

There was a great dichotomy between town and village life. As evacuees' accounts attested later, there were some prosperous, middle-class families in Petersfield who could afford one or more servants, usually housemaids, although some even boasted cooks, parlour maids and butlers too. (This caused some surprise to one London evacuee who wrote to his parents that his host family had 'men waitresses'!) Other families, especially those in the outlying villages, however, lived in what contemporary Londoners would have called primitive conditions.

Girls who found themselves in service may or may not have been treated well, but they were glad of a paid position in hard times. Gladys Turner made good friends among the staff where she worked at Island in Steep, but understandably rebelled against the injustice or ill-treatment she received at the hands of the butler. Hierarchies were important in those days.

The 1930s were a hard time for Gladys Betteridge too. She and her husband had moved to Queens Road in 1932 (she still lives there today), but money was very scarce with a son, the deposit on the house, and her husband (a baker) earning only 25s a week, a third of which went towards the mortgage. Enterprise sometimes paid off: both David Martin's and Vic Walker's parents had survived the 1930s by running itinerant businesses, Mr Martin senior delivering groceries and paraffin, Mr and Mrs Walker senior selling fruit and vegetables and making a success of it.

Buriton and Sheet are examples of villages where families existed without mains drainage until the mid-1930s. Clive Ellis remembers the weekly sewage collection in Sheet by the 'ghost cart' of George Money, when all wise people kept their windows

Petersfield Square in the 1930s, with Norman Burton's on the north side. (Petersfield Museum)

Petersfield Square, east side, in the 1930s. (Petersfield Museum)

The Town Hall on its completion in 1935. (Petersfield Museum)

tightly shut! It was not until 1936 that inside toilets were installed in Sheet houses. Village Street, then known as Sheet Street, was also known as 'soapsud alley' owing to the open drain which ran down the side of the street and took away the sink waste. On Mondays (washing day) it became white with foam.

For the parents of Don and Phil Eades in Buriton, it was 'the old way of life': their mother worked from morning till night cooking, washing and cleaning. Water was heated in a copper with a wood fire beneath it; the toilet was an earth-closet at the end of the garden and once a week there was a visit from the gentlemen with 'the violet wagon'!

The 1930s saw the construction of a spate of both public and private buildings in Petersfield. In 1935 a new cinema, the Savoy, was built by Solly Filer to replace his old Electric cinema; the same year saw the completion of the new Town Hall, comprising a large and a small hall used for concerts, dances, plays and meetings of many kinds. Boots the Chemist came to the High Street in 1936; the Wesleyan church (now the Masonic Hall) followed in 1937, and over the course of that decade the Bell Hill estate, the Causeway and Woodbury Avenue were constructed. All these buildings, still in existence today, bear the distinctive architectural style of the period.

One building that disappeared during the course of the 1930s was the brewery in College Street, which had been in the Luker family since the early nineteenth-century. This family also owned or subsequently bought the Red Lion, the Dolphin Hotel, the Railway Hotel, the Market Inn, the Good Intent, the Harrow Inn in Steep and the Queen's Head in Sheet. Shortly after the brewery was sold to Filer, the Portsmouth property developer and cinema owner, it was destroyed by fire in 1934, and the site, with the original tower demolished because the fire had rendered it unsafe, remained a demolition site until after the war. The neglected Antrobus Almshouses, dating from the seventeenth century and immediately adjacent to the brewery, also stood derelict in College Street during the war years.

Naturally, to different generations, the thirties represented different things. To schoolchildren, it evokes a time when discipline was strict, with severe punishments for misbehaviour: it was not at all uncommon for boys and girls to be caned for getting their sums wrong, for rulers to be smacked across children's knuckles, or for two children's heads to be banged together if they were caught talking in class. It has frequently been mooted that this severity towards schoolchildren was probably the result of schools being run as Dame schools by the 'tribes of elderly spinsters' (as David Scurfield has called them) who either had not been able to get married in the first place (as a result of the loss of men in the First World War), or had been widowed young, or had simply retired from teaching years before. They were still the Victorian generation operating Victorian values, educated but pedagogically démodé, available but unequal to the task of educating youngsters in the later 1930s.

To housewives, it was a time when they could order goods in a shop and have them delivered the same day; since shops in Petersfield were, by and large, family-run businesses, they showed courtesy, even deference, to their customers. Like many provincial towns, Petersfield was experiencing the golden age of the small shopkeeper. Victorian values of industriousness, self-help and individual enterprise were the foundations for the rise of those self-made men, the proud owners of small shops. Being a shopkeeper was very much a way of life and shop owners, together with their families who lived over the shops, were close-knit communities. A large

The new Savoy cinema, with Flora Twort's shop (1 The Square) on the right. (Petersfield Museum)

percentage of these small shops passed down the family from generation to generation and many of the children of the different shopkeepers grew up together.

Meanwhile, for the moneyed classes, there were servants, fine houses and leisure to
enjoy; the Hambledon Foxhounds and their Master, the Petersfield Squire, Sam Hardy,
met on the green in The Spain; and winter holidays abroad were not unknown.

The aspects of the town which cannot be recorded in print are the sounds and
smells which must have characterised it three-quarters of a century ago: the cattle
at the market, the smell of warm bread from the numerous bakeries in the town,
the Salvation Army band playing in The Square, the clatter of the printing presses
in Childs' High Street offices, the lowing of the cattle in the meadows at the edge of
town, the steam engines puffing across the viaduct at Ramshill, the aroma from the
hopkilns at Weston, the horses at the Taro Fair each October, the swish of skaters
on the Pond in the frozen winters, the clanking of the aerial wire systems for cash
payments in certain shops, the wildlife – especially the birds – on the Heath. It is
interesting to note that the official town guide for 1938 records 110 species of birds
which had been sighted in the vicinity of Petersfield. Perhaps 'progress' has been at
the expense of such delights and we are living in a more clinical, less sensory, age?

A theme which constantly recurs among the older residents of Petersfield when
talking of the pre-war days is the sheer, unadulterated, safe, rural freedom enjoyed by
contemporary children. They paddled in the Heath Pond (despite its muddy bottom),

The old Railway Hotel which was demolished in the early 1980s. It is now the site of Lavant Court.
(Petersfield Museum)

Childs' stationers, home of the Hants and Sussex News, *the* Squeaker. *(Petersfield Museum)*

E. J. BAKER,

PURVEYOR OF

❧ ❧ MEAT, ❧ ❧

Fishmonger, Poulterer and
Licensed Dealer in Game.

ESTABLISHED 1787.

High St., Petersfield
And at GRANGE FARM.

Advert for E.J. Baker from the official town brochure of 1938.(Author's Collection)

PETERSFIELD AND DISTRICT.

Mr. W. P. JACOBS, F.A.I.,

Auctioneer, Valuer and Surveyor,

LAND, HOUSE, ESTATE & INSURANCE AGENT.

Sales of Farm Stock, Timber, Household Furniture, Freehold and other Properties, undertaken at Moderate Charges.

Valuations for Probate and Estate Duty.   Inventories Taken and Checked.

Sales of Fat and Store Stock held in Petersfield Market every alternate Wednesday throughout the year.

SPACIOUS SALE ROOMS AND STORAGE ACCOMMODATION.

Offices and Sale Rooms :

LAVANT STREET, PETERSFIELD.

Telegrams : "JACOBS, PETERSFIELD."   Telephone No.

W. DUFFETT,

Watchmaker and Jeweller.

WATCHES, CLOCKS, BAROMETERS,
WEDDING, ENGAGEMENT and DRESS RINGS.

Silver and Electro-plated Goods.   Presentation Plate.
Old Gold and Silver Bought and Exchanged.

High Street, PETERSFIELD.

Adverts for businesses from the official town brochure for 1938. (Author's Collection)

they skated (and cycled!) on its ice in winter, they played in the streams and meadows, walked for miles (often alone), created dens and caves in the sandy banks of Dark Hollow or Sheet Common 'ravine', or climbed and swung on trees out of view and earshot of their parents. In short, they invented their own entertainments outside the home without incurring the anxiety or wrath of the adult world.

Much of this carefree idyll was brought to an abrupt halt, however, with the Munich Crisis of 1938. Hitler's first attempt to unite Germany and Austria ended in the failed coup of 1934; four years later the new Austrian Chancellor, Artur von Seyss-Inquart, leader of the Austrian Nazi Party, invited Hitler to occupy his country and the *Anschluss* (Hitler's annexation of Austria to Germany) became a reality in March 1938. In then demanding the return of the Sudetenland to Germany, which had been ceded to Czechoslovakia by the Treaty of Versailles in 1918, Hitler benefited from the great desire for peace among Germany's erstwhile enemies and they acquiesced to his demand and signed the Munich Agreement in September 1938. The future began to look bleak as the appeasers' optimism faded with the takeover of the whole of Czechoslovakia by Hitler the following March; protests from many quarters, however, did not lead to any action being taken, let alone any solution being found. Hitler's next move, the invasion of Poland on 1 September 1939, sealed the fate of Europe for the next six years.

CHAPTER ONE

1939

The First Evacuees

NATIONAL SERVICE

In January 1939 His Majesty's Stationery Office issued a booklet to every household outlining the types of voluntary work available for people to help answer the call to national service. The Prime Minister, Neville Chamberlain, wrote this foreword:

> The desire of all of us is to live at peace with our neighbours. But to ensure peace we must be strong. The Country needs your services and you are anxious to play your part. This Guide will point the way. I ask you to read it carefully and to decide how you can best help.

National service could take many forms: people may have been choosing a career for the first time, or looking for a new career. The traditional form of active service in the Royal Navy, Army or Air Force or the alternatives, the regular Police Forces or Fire Brigades, were strongly promoted. For those already engaged in work vital to the country's security, this could be considered national service in itself. There were also numerous possibilities for carrying out full- or part-time service in wartime which could serve as training for a peacetime job afterwards. The booklet explained the openings available in the auxiliary fighting services such as the Royal Naval Volunteer Reserve, the Territorial Army, the Royal Air Force Volunteer Reserve and the Auxiliary Air Force. These were mainly aimed at younger men, but older men could join the ARP (Air Raid Precautions) as wardens, ambulance drivers or communications experts, for example, or the Special Constabulary or the Observer Corps. For women, there were jobs similar to those for older men, with the alternative occupations in the Auxiliary Hospital Service or the Women's Land Army, for example. Mavis Brett joined the AFS (Auxiliary Fire Service) and, like many women of her generation who took what had previously been thought of as 'men's jobs', she found the skills she learnt invaluable in later life.

In fact, the ARP had already been mobilised during the Munich Crisis and some 38 million gasmasks had been delivered to households by September 1938. During the war, schoolchildren found having to carry the cardboard boxes containing their gas masks rather tedious; at school the boxes kept falling off chairs in classrooms or getting kicked around.

In February 1939 the government announced plans to distribute Anderson shelters. Made of steel and tunnel-shaped, these were to be erected in people's gardens. By September that same year about 2 million had already been issued.

PREPARATIONS IN PETERSFIELD

By the middle of the hot summer of 1939 Petersfield appeared to be prepared for the war which now seemed imminent: civil defence exercises and air raid precautions were under way, and blackout practices were being held under the direction of the ARP organiser Mr R.H. Caplen. Consignments of tinned meat had already begun arriving at the railway station ready for the evacuees leaving London for Petersfield and who were to be supervised by the Rural District Council's Chief Billeting Officer, Mr W.R. Gates. Meanwhile, some boys from Churcher's College were taken by local builders' lorries to the large sandpit in Borough Road, now the recreation ground, where they spent hours filling the sandbags which were used to protect public buildings in Petersfield such as the Town Hall, the post office, the police station, the churches and the banks. This work had previously started in the hot August of 1938, continuing through 1939, even before war had been declared. Mary Ray had already been attending first-aid lectures with her mother, who had joined the Civil Defence organisation as a first-aider.

A census of all babies and small children was in the process of being drawn up so that respirators (gas masks) and protective helmets could be issued with speed and efficiency. The Fire Brigades Committee reported that it currently had one 500 gallons-per-minute and two 120 gallons-per-minute pumps and recommended the purchase of a Dennis Light-Four fire engine to supplement the one it already possessed. This was agreed by the Petersfield Urban District Council.

Below: Some identity badges of the voluntary services. (Chris Lloyd Collection)

Right: Armbands for the voluntary services. (Chris Lloyd Collection)

Royal Tank Corps on manoeuvres near Petersfield in 1938. (Imperial War Museum)

In private households, people made their own preparations for war. Many families started by using their cupboards under the stairs to shelter in; the Burley family converted a downstairs toilet into a mini air-raid shelter and, after moving to a larger house in Bell Hill, they transformed the dining room into a purpose-built shelter for the whole family where they slept and ate throughout the war.

In May 1939 the government's proposals for dispersing the population in the event of war were published. The scheme envisaged the division of the country into 'danger' areas (from which evacuation was recommended), 'neutral' areas (where no movement was permitted), and 'safe' or 'reception' areas (which included Petersfield). Each area contained roughly a third of the total population of the country. In the 'safe' areas, Billeting Officers were already drawing up lists of potential hosts for the expected arrivals.

THE OUTBREAK OF WAR

On 1 September 1939 Mary Ray remembers being with a friend in a house in the High Street when it was announced that Hitler had invaded Poland. This caused consternation among the adults present and made the young teenagers realise that something momentous was about to happen. Sunday 3 September 1939, the day war broke out, Shirley George was in Steep with her family, who were stunned into silence by the announcement. Ted Baigent was at Sunday school and came home to hear the Prime Minister, Neville Chamberlain's announcement of Britain's state of war with Germany. Jenny Dandridge started dancing round the garden because she and her friends thought that the war was going to be fun, while in Sheet, April

Austin was performing handstands with her friend Barbara Todd in the garden of the Harlequin café, next to the Half Moon pub, where her mother worked. From the wireless at the open window of the café came Mr Chamberlain's message, striking alarm into the listeners. At Sheet church that morning, some of the girls from Portsmouth High School evacuated at nearby Adhurst St Mary gasped when the vicar announced the news of war and they ran out of the church crying. Margaret Childs was standing in her parents' bedroom in School Lane, Sheet, when she heard the neighbour telling her father that war had been declared: she looked out over the meadow and wondered if she might see Germans approaching at any moment. . . .

In a similar example of immediate panic, John Freeman remembers the feverish activity the day after war was declared, when Council workers began digging trenches on the Heath; however, these were never used or manned during the war. The eight-year-old John Lovell had been left for safety with a cousin and a maid in the family's newly purchased, but incomplete, house in The Causeway, where building work was still under way. Unbeknown to his parents, the builders had left a gas pipe unplugged, and if it had not been for the windows being left open on that warm September night, John might not be alive today!

In St Peter's church, where the vicar, the Revd E.C.A. Kent, was preaching, the congregation included a number of children and teachers from Emanuel School, Wandsworth Common, in London, who had already started arriving in the town. Among those who had first greeted the new arrivals was Revd Kent himself who,

Children's gasmasks. (Chris Lloyd Collection)

A child's protective suit for gas raids. (Chris Lloyd Collection)

by a happy coincidence, was the former curate in their London parish.

Soon afterwards, gas masks were distributed to a frightened population. Children were issued with gas masks in cardboard boxes – the girls used to make smart little coloured cases to cover them – and gas mask drills started.

According to the *Hants and Sussex News*, affectionately known to all as the '*Squeaker*', the great exodus from London – well over half a million people had already left the capital – was causing 'a disturbing and lasting effect on the life of the community'. As in the rest of the country, the limitation on movement brought about by lighting and traffic restrictions and the large increase in the populations of rural districts, caused by the influx of thousands of children and their mothers from city areas, began to alter the face of Petersfield from the very beginning of the war. The four-day scramble to find homes for the first newcomers had been a testing time for the Chief Evacuation Officer, Colonel W.R. Beazley and his team, but, thanks to their efficiency, had produced satisfactory results. Assistance had been provided by the Women's VAD (Voluntary Aid Detachment), the police and the Boy Scouts. While waiting to be taken to their billets, some children remained in St Peter's church while others were taken to the Petersfield Senior Council School (the present Petersfield Junior School in St Peter's Road). In a letter published by the *Squeaker*, the Second Master of Emanuel School, Mr W. Stafford Hipkins, expressed 'the very real gratitude felt towards the inhabitants of Petersfield for their amazingly cordial welcome'.

The *Squeaker* of 20 September carried the already universally familiar message:

WALLS HAVE EARS!

There is too much talking! Information which might be of great value to the enemy is being passed on every day in hotels, public houses, and general meeting places.

Soldiers, sailors, and airmen are forbidden to talk shop – why should you?

It is every citizen's duty to refrain from discussing with their friends such information as movements and numbers of troops and the names and nature of units and stations.

The enemy has a spy system. Chance remarks are often dangerous. Failure to comply with this request may result in severe penalties.

STOP TALKING!

FRANK CARPENTER & THE SQUEAKER

Frank Carpenter was born in Petersfield in 1871. From the British School, next to the Congregational church in College Street (now the United Reformed church), he won a scholarship to Churcher's College, where he stayed from 1883 to 1886. His first jobs were clerical; later, he began to report meetings and debates, and his career in journalism had begun.

When he started, everything was handwritten and then set in type by hand. The telephone was not available and a bicycle was his only means of transport other than foot. He became editor of the *Hants and Sussex News* at the age of twenty and remained with the paper for fifty-six years, retiring in 1947. His career as a journalist stretched from the days when it was customary to write column-length reports of every local meeting to the time when brevity and condensation, as well as accuracy, became the hallmark of journalism.

During the war the *Squeaker* (the *Hants and Sussex News*) was a four-page broadsheet, costing 1d (this rose to 1½d by the end of the war). The front page was devoted to reports of meetings of the two Petersfield District Councils, of Petersfield Petty Sessions, and to major local (and sometimes national) events. It was not unusual to read in great detail the events surrounding a local wedding or a school Speech Day. The second page consisted almost entirely of small adverts or larger, boxed advertisements placed by local shopkeepers and notices of forthcoming events; pages three and four contained more in-depth news, articles, and, occasionally, letters from readers. There were no photographs and very few illustrated advertisements; nor was there any editorial comment. However, Frank Carpenter's own elegant English and professionally accurate style were usually detectable in the articles.

Although his life's work was spent in Petersfield, his was not a career without event. He saw the trend in election meetings change from the time when rotten tomatoes were hurled at candidates to the more sedate meetings of the 1945 general election. He sympathised with the Votes for Women movement and was a friend of Sylvia Pankhurst, the suffragette leader; he even had to confront a crowd of virulent anti-feminists outside

St Peter's vicarage when Mrs Pankhurst was present at a meeting with the vicar.

Frank Carpenter played a vigorous part in the life of Petersfield; in a unique way he became part of the local scene, being the one man everybody knew and who knew almost everybody. His knowledge of Petersfield personalities and local history was also unique; he was his own reporter, sub-editor, commentator and local historian, and editor. People used to say that there were two really permanent features of the town: the King William statue, and Frank Carpenter.

For nearly fifty years he was connected with the Petersfield Literary and Debating Society and was one of its vice-presidents; he was secretary of the Working Men's Institute for more than twenty years; he was a self-taught musician, playing the organ and the piano with equal facility, as well as the violin and cello. He was also a keen sportsman and used to play both football and cricket for the town, being captain of the football club and its secretary for many years.

He died in 1960, in his ninetieth year, and over a hundred people crowded into St Peter's church for his funeral service. In his address the vicar, Revd J.S. Long, called Frank Carpenter a man of integrity and uprightness with an innate kindness of heart, who had been content to spend the whole of a long working life serving the people of his native town which he loved so dearly.

Frank Carpenter. (Author's Collection)

THE HOME GUARD

At the beginning of the war, there was a great burst of patriotism and enthusiasm among young people to perform some service within the community. The formation of the new LDV (Local Defence Volunteers) had begun in May 1940 in immediate response to a broadcast by the then Secretary of State for War, Anthony Eden. These units, which were later to become the Home Guard, were issued initially with a simple armband. Many of them had no weapons at all, but later they received obsolete rifles and a small amount of ammunition. Their role was to guard various strategic spots, prepare for a potential invasion and keep a general watch for paratroopers landing. In Petersfield, their duties amounted to guarding the Buriton and Privett railway tunnel entrances on the main line from London to Portsmouth; manning the concrete road blocks which had been set up by the Forebridge at the bottom of the Causeway, at the junction of Bell Hill and the Winchester road, and in Ramshill; keeping watch on key establishments in the area, and remaining in general readiness by attending drill sessions and military exercises several times a week. They were also taken to the Langrish range for rifle-shooting practice. The road blocks consisted partly of permanent concrete blocks, 5ft high and sunk into the ground with iron girders at the sides of the roadway, and partly of other blocks kept to one side to be lifted by crane into place across the road in the event of an invasion.

Vic Walker, in the Churcher's OTC (Officer Training Corps) at this time, remembers his father, who had served in the Navy in the First World War, asking for instruction in army matters. Likewise, Margaret Childs' father, who had learnt gunnery in the First World War, became an instructor for the Home Guard. Churcher's College played an important role here: the senior NCOs in the school were employed at the Drill Hall in Dragon Street (subsequently demolished and the site now occupied by The Maltings) to train the Home Guard in drill, disciplinary matters and rough tactics on Field Days. This led to a few problems because the masters who had joined the Home Guard did not take kindly to being shouted at by their pupils! One such unfortunate master was told on parade one day that he looked like a 'lopsided marrow' at which he complained to the Headmaster about his treatment! In general, however, the Home Guard probably benefited from the semi-trained OTC.

The Commander of the Petersfield Home Guard was Captain, later Colonel, Charles, who had been gassed in the First World War and who, despite some deafness, was a French teacher at Churcher's College.

A certain Captain Chambers had been sent to Petersfield to help with Home Guard training and coordinate transport for services in the area; he had a centre in Dragon Street, opposite the Drill Hall. On one occasion, a Spitfire had shot down a Messerschmitt at Harting and a private from the RAFC was sent over to stand guard at the scene. On returning to Petersfield to report the incident to Captain Chambers, his superior, he said he had 'found' a Luger pistol in the plane; Chambers demanded the pistol, took it but accidentally pulled the trigger and shot the private in the leg. Vic Walker recounts how, forty years later, in an antique shop in East Grinstead, he met the private in question who claimed the unique distinction of being 'wounded in action in Petersfield'!

John Freeman joined the Home Guard at the age of seventeen and took part in regular training sessions which were held at the Drill Hall in Dragon Street or behind the Town Hall. Firing practice took place on the Bordon ranges. The main bases to be guarded were at Churcher's College (by the petrol station), at the Welcome Inn, now the site of Meon Close (protecting the coal supplies), and at the Town Hall. The Home Guard mounted guard at both ends of Butser railway tunnel, a vital link for movements between London and Portsmouth. On the top of Butser itself was a Forestry Commission fire tower, which provided an excellent viewing point for detecting any parachutists in the area, and a wireless station for radioing messages to the ARP and other authorities. (The original military use for Butser Hill was the semaphore, which connected the Admiralty in London with Portsmouth Naval Base.) There were firing ranges in an old quarry on the road between Buriton and Butser Hill. Emanuel School JTC (Junior Training Corps) even had a Field Day on Butser during the war. Roy Barrow remembers his father talking of being in the Home Guard and crossing the main railway line wearing a greatcoat which, when dripping wet, was likely to touch the unprotected live rail. With a rifle in one hand and holding the greatcoat up around his knees, stepping across the line became a test of nerve in itself.

On another occasion, to test the Home Guard's preparedness, a dummy attack on the Town Hall took place. David Scurfield remembers being terrified out of his wits – and nearly out of his pram – by the dive-bombing planes and the exploding dummy bombs, until the Home Guard arrived to control the situation.

The Welcome Inn, now Meon Close. (Petersfield Museum)

George Cook joined the Steep platoon, which consisted of between twenty-five and thirty volunteers, and every ten days or so they would take a night duty (four hours on, four hours off). They had an observation post on Stoner Hill, watching out for potential parachutists landing.

Clive Ellis remembers the moment after the fall of France in 1940 when Colonel Paul Maze, who had escaped the German Occupation of France, crossed to England in his car and settled in Steep. He was a friend of Winston Churchill's cousin Lord Ivor Spencer Churchill who lived at Little Langley's. As a well-known artist of the First World War, he had taught Winston Churchill to paint. Colonel Maze later generously gave his car to the Petersfield Home Guard, who used it to transport their patrols to the Butser cutting. It was probably thanks to the Churchill connection that the unit seems to have been well supplied with arms – heavy French machine guns, for example!

EVACUEE SCHOOL ARRIVALS

Unsurprisingly, it was the schoolchildren who felt the greatest impact of the war on their daily lives. Two major schools, Emanuel School and Battersea Central School, for boys and girls respectively, found refuge in the town, both operating a shift system for teaching purposes. Two other schools, Portsmouth High School (girls) and West Mark Camp School (mixed), were reconstituted in Sheet in order to provide safety for children whose family homes were in Portsmouth. In addition to all these changes, there was an impact felt in the town's Junior and Senior Schools (in St Peter's Road), either from the influx of the younger siblings of the evacuated schoolchildren into normal classes, or from their need to share their premises with the newcomers. This disruption was also felt – albeit to a lesser extent – in the local village schools in Steep and Sheet, which were attended by some evacuee children.

(a) Churcher's College and Emanuel School

The first great movement of schoolchildren from London at the outbreak of war had to synchronise with the troop movements caused by the despatch of the British Expeditionary Force to France. Hampshire was particularly affected because, not only were military units being rushed through Portsmouth at this time, but Overton in Hampshire was accommodating departments of the Bank of England and Dunbridge was the centre for a huge American depot. The evacuation of children was a priority, however, and was organised down to the smallest detail; on 1, 2 and 3 September trains for evacuating children out of London were not available for ordinary passengers. The whole operation during those first three days of September represented by far the largest organised mass movement of civilians ever undertaken in Great Britain.

At first, the boys of Emanuel School from Battersea, in the London Borough of Wandsworth, had absolutely no idea of where they were being sent. They had spent

FREQUENT
ELECTRIC TRAINS
and Cheap Fares to
PETERSFIELD
From LONDON (Waterloo) daily.
Seats reserved (1/-) in principal services.

CHEAP FARES from LONDON
" MONTHLY RETURN " Tickets issued daily,
available for any period within **A MONTH.**

1st Class	3rd Class
14/8	9/9

Ask for pamphlet at S.R. Stations.

·········· When on Holiday ··········
SEE THE DISTRICT !
by taking advantage of the CHEAP DAY TICKETS issued from
PETERSFIELD by ALL trains daily, as under :—

CHICHESTER ...2/11	MIDHURST ... 1/7
(Weds. only)	PORTSMOUTH
GUILDFORD ... 3/5	& SOUTHSEA 2/8
HAVANT ...1/10	PORTSMOUTH
HAYLING	HARBOUR ...2/11
ISLAND 2/4	RYDE
LISS ... ...5½d.	ESPLANADE 4/6

Also to LONDON (Wednesdays and Thursdays only) by all trains
after 8.30 a.m., 7/4
Available for return on day of issue by any train.

For full particulars of Train Services, Cheap Tickets, etc., apply at local
S.R. Stations, or to Traffic Manager (Commercial Superintendent), Southern
Railway, London Bridge Station, S.E.1.

SOUTHERN ELECTRIC
Quickest way to Sunshine

*Train services to and from Petersfield and
London, from a 1938 brochure. (Author's
Collection)*

*The Square in wartime, with the old Commercial
Hotel and weighbridge. (Petersfield Museum)*

most of their summer holiday that year anticipating a departure, then had been told to report to their school every day during the last week of August, and finally, on Friday 1 September, they were marched directly to Clapham Junction station. On the platform a friend of Dennis Geen, who worked for the railway, tapped him on the shoulder with the words: 'You're going to Petersfield. I shall tell your mother.' But the Emanuel boys were no wiser with this piece of news until they consulted the Southern Railway map in their compartment, located Petersfield, and knew their fate.

Phyllis White remembered standing on the footbridge of Petersfield station awaiting the arrival of the 'little boys from London' – some of whom turned out to be six feet tall, making difficulties for families in small homes! A few Boy Scouts also stood waiting on the platform to act as their escorts into town.

When they arrived they were marched down Lavant Street into St Peter's church for a short break, thence to the Junior Council School next door (now demolished and part of St Peter's Court) where the Billeting Officer allocated their billets and introduced their host families to them. Thanks to the warm, dry weather that September, the first three weeks spent organising the new routines for the Emanuel boys – the school met in the Petersfield Junior School playground to plan each day – passed without hitches. Indeed, the time was valuably spent in performing such tasks as filling sandbags, picking hops, docking marigolds or tedding hay. In fact, the Emanuel boys had begun to share their scholastic base with Bedales, but this proved to be awkward, given the two schools' distinctly different approaches to education, and the more formally educated Emanuel boys joined with Churcher's College in late September. One of the first tasks for the boys from both Churcher's and Emanuel was to dig air-raid shelters on Heath Harrison Field at Churcher's, to be used as shelters during lesson time. These were trenches, zigzag in shape to avoid blast damage, with corrugated iron roofs and the excavated soil placed on top. Steve Pibworth remembers being asked to take to school a small tin with cotton wool (for the ears) and an India rubber (to put between the teeth) to prevent injury during a bombing raid!

Churcher's College (at the time a voluntary-aided grammar school) held classes in the mornings, while the Emanuel boys occupied the same premises in the afternoons. The remaining half-day for each set of pupils was taken up with additional classes elsewhere in town, on the sports field, or in training exercises for the schools' OTC contingents. It was inevitable that some members of staff would be called up and in some cases this led to a shortage of subject teachers: Buster Hampton, for example, remembers being unable to study biology because of this. He and a group of Churcherians, who had been following the training afforded by the Petersfield Squadron of the ATC (Air Training Corps) after school, also aimed to go to Cambridge University, not to study, but to join the Air Force quickly via the University Air Squadron. By this means, they could save the six to twelve weeks' initial training period. It was possible in the wartime to leave school after one year in the Sixth Form and, true to the spirit of commitment of the period, many Churcherians 'disappeared' into the Services.

On Saturdays the Emanuel First XV played on a field near Lord's Farm in Steep. (To play 'rugby at Lord's' seemed incongruous, but amusing!) Curiously, the farm is owned today by John Lovell, a rare Petersfield 'Old Emanuel boy', who had joined the school in early 1941 because Churcher's College was full. In practice, with the alternating system of morning or afternoon sports, Churcher's playing fields could easily accommodate the large number of Emanuel boys, except for some inter-school matches in the afternoons. However, this was not the case with classrooms, and supplementary space had to be found in the town in an improbable combination of premises: the Town Hall, the Working Men's Institute (now the Petersfield Social Club), the Blue Anchor (opposite Churcher's, on the present site of the entrance to Hoggarth Way), Windsor Road Methodist chapel (now the Masonic Hall) and the Sun Inn (now the Green Dragon), the latter also serving as the school bookstore and as a base for 'the man from Harrods' for their school uniforms and other requirements. A Harrods representative, a certain Mr Fennel, came down to Petersfield every Wednesday throughout the war with a mobile shop to take orders from Emanuel pupils and staff. One master even bought a piano there; unfortunately it was too large to go through the front door of his billet, so Harrods supplied a smaller one the following week!

The Sun Inn, now the Green Dragon. (Petersfield Museum)

The order of the day was for shared premises, and boys and girls alike from the various schools in the town went to Churcher's College for their chemistry laboratories or to Bedales for their biology laboratory, their library and the use of their swimming pool. As Vaughan Clarke has commented: 'Possibly the hardiest travellers were the biologists of the Emanuel School Sixth Form, under the direction of Mr T.E. Hughes, for they walked to Bedales two afternoons a week, whatever the weather, to use the laboratory.'

The town seethed with schoolchildren (mainly boys) in the daytime and, later, with troops in the evenings and at weekends. The Churcher's and Emanuel contingents remained firmly apart, with each set of boys going to school up and down different sides of Ramshill. Initially, both sets of pupils made their way across town to the venues allocated to their various classes, but this inefficiency was redressed when it was decided that the teachers should do the moving. This clearly led to some scurrying around the town by the teachers, but the most difficult problem was the logistical one – how to warn boys of changes to their timetables. Aeron Rogers, the senior maths master, solved this by sending out chits (memos) via a small boy on a bicycle!

Roy Maxwell remembers his schooldays at Emanuel as well disciplined; Mr Broom, the Headmaster, was an impressive character who knew every boy by name and he and his wife exerted a restraining influence on the boys who swarmed around the town in their free time. The Harrods uniform, black herring-bone suits with short trousers, school cap and gabardine raincoat in the winter and a boater in the summer, was easily identifiable – indeed, the boater became the mark of an ex-Petersfield evacuee after the war when Emanuel boys returned to London.

Lou Crosswell's first experiences as an evacuee were not auspicious: he had to move billets three times before settling into a house in Inman Terrace in Sheet. One of the first houses he found himself in had no sanitation, the chicken shed at the end of the garden serving as a lavatory. In between moves he went to the hostel run by Mr Stafford Hipkins, Emanuel's Second Master and the master delegated to oversee all billeting problems during the evacuation years. This hostel, situated at 60 Heath Road and run by a Mrs Booth, helped boys in 'difficult' billets to re-adjust to new ones. In Lou's final house in Sheet there was no bathroom, so on a Friday evening the boiler was stoked up and filled and the three members of the household (he, his hostess, and her 80-year-old mother) each had a bath in turn in the kitchen! However, Lou was well looked after; he had his own room, did his homework on the kitchen table and ate fresh vegetables from the garden – where there was a large quince tree providing quince pie for lunch on Sundays. Many children from that part of Sheet used to congregate in a field at the end of their road next to the Half Moon and play football or cricket.

A very small number of boys at Emanuel had not originally been pupils at the school; having attended other schools in London, they subsequently gained scholarships to Emanuel and, naturally, were transferred to Petersfield. Charles Sammonds, for example, came down to Hampshire along with his other schoolmates from Battersea Central (Boys) School, a third of whom (about eighty boys) were evacuated to the area around Hawkley, Empshott, Greatham, Newton Valence and Liss, the remainder going to Rowlands Castle. He then won a County Scholarship, but remained in Empshott from 1940 until 1944 and cycled every day the 7½ miles to Churcher's and back. He found the transition from the strong cockney working-class ethos of his Battersea school to the mainly middle-class or local Hampshire culture quite confusing. In addition to this social upheaval, he arrived at Churcher's at fourteen years of age and had to work doubly hard and doubly fast to catch up with his contemporaries. He was also embarrassed by the expense of his new school uniform (supplied by Harrods) and it took his father, who earned 35s a week, eighteen months to repay it at half-a-crown a week. By the time his County clothing grant came through by his first Christmas, he felt less incongruous as he was at last able to afford his first pair of long trousers!

From the Emanuel School point of view, the initial adjustment to life in Petersfield families seems to have been rather chaotic, but this was primarily due to the fact that the Hampshire County Council, to whom all responsibility had been delegated, gave higher priority to its own schools in Portsmouth and Southampton than to the Londoners. It must be stressed that, had it not been for the fortunate compatibility between the two headmasters concerned, Mr Hoggarth, of Churcher's, and Mr Broom, of Emanuel, and the efforts of Mr Hipkins (of Emanuel) and Mr A.J. Wilkins (of the Urban District Council), the problems would have persisted far longer. It took approximately three weeks, including the time to bring the 15 tons of scholastic equipment from London, before the school became properly operative.

Emanuel School held their assemblies every Monday morning in St Peter's church. The unity and *esprit de corps* created by the semblance of normality, which was made possible by the evacuation to Petersfield, certainly helped Emanuel achieve the academic success it had been used to before the war. For those who fell prey to homesickness, there was one weekend *exeat* available each half-term – all they had to do was to persuade their last teacher on a Friday afternoon to let them go early so that they could rush to the station for the 5.15 train to London!

(b) Petersfield County High School for Girls and Battersea Central School for Girls

An almost identical situation was experienced by the girls of Battersea Central School, about 50 per cent of whom also left Clapham Junction for an unknown destination, armed with carrier bags and gas masks. On arrival in Petersfield, they were shepherded to the Junior Council School in St Peter's Road and given refreshments, including half a pound of chocolate! Unlike the Emanuel boys, some of the Battersea girls were 'selected' for billets by their hosts who fetched them directly from the school hall, while others went in a crocodile through the town and waited for the Billeting Officer to knock on people's doors to see if they would or could be accepted. Some of the girls were placed with families in Liss and had

Petersfield County High School for Girls, 1951, now Dolphin Court. Miss Dorothy Chadwick, the Headmistress, is second from the right. (Petersfield Museum)

to catch a bus to school in Petersfield each day. Again, the experiences of each pair of girls billeted in the town were varied: those who were considered the most fortunate found themselves in large houses overlooking the Heath, sometimes sharing their accommodation and their dining facilities with the live-in maids which many middle-class families had in those days. Noreen Stocker was billeted in a house right beside the embankment of the Midhurst railway line which, when the workhouse bomb fell in November 1940, saved the house from considerable damage and herself from injury.

As far as school classes were concerned, the Battersea girls began by sharing the premises of Petersfield County High School in the old Dolphin Hotel building (now the Dolphin Court site) at the corner of the High Street and Dragon Street. Later, some of the Battersea girls had classes in Hylton House (more recently, Moreton

House), which relieved the pressure on space at the County High School. Again, as with Churcher's and Emanuel, the 'home' pupils used the High Street premises in the mornings, the visitors in the afternoons, with extra activities throughout the town for both groups to fill the day. There were even a dozen or so under elevens, younger brothers and sisters of the Battersea girls, who had an improvised education from essentially secondary-level teachers. Like the other evacuated schools in Petersfield, they found themselves using *ad hoc* accommodation – the YWCA garden (behind Winton House), the Red Lion, the Methodist hall, the Congregational (United Reform) church hall, the Town Hall council chamber and even the boiler room of the old workhouse when a siren sounded! The school used the Methodist hall every Tuesday for its assemblies. Many lifelong friendships resulted from the evacuation, of course, and five Battersea girls have never forgotten the welcome received from Admiral and Mrs Hugh Miller who housed them.

Logistically, the Girls' High School presented enormous problems to the two sets of pupils who were to inhabit it for the duration of the war. The building had all but been condemned as unsuitable and insufficient in size before the war and Miss Chadwick, the recently appointed Headmistress, was wont to describe it as

A classroom in Petersfield County Girls' School. (Petersfield Museum)

'the slum property of the Hampshire Education Committee'. With the influx of the Londoners, it began, almost literally, to groan. Not only were there double the number of pupils there had been before the war, but each school's numbers increased steadily as children from outside the area came to stay with aunts or grandparents in the relative safety of Petersfield. In Mary Ray's class alone there were eight such newcomers. April Austin remembers the building 'shivering and shaking' when the Petersfield girls all left their classrooms at midday. In fact, the demolition of what Mary Ray has described as 'this nice, rickety, noisy old building', the former Dolphin Hotel (which prior to that had been the Dolphin Inn and originally the Red Lion Inn dating from the 1660s), did not happen until 1965.

Mary Ray particularly remembers a European history lesson she attended in another premises used by the school (now Folly Fires): the then main A3 road (Dragon Street) was narrower at that point and some of the girls in the overcrowded room were sitting on the window seat as tracked vehicles of the Canadian Army rumbled past and drowned the teacher's voice. On other occasions, the girls experienced some wolf-whistling from the Royal Engineers, who had taken over the workshops of Britnell and Crawters garage (now the Folly Market), as they passed by on their way from school assembly to their main classroom in the Congregational church hall.

Numerically, the visitors far outnumbered the 'home' pupils: there were approximately 450 Emanuel School boys, compared with 283 at Churcher's College, and the 250 black and yellow uniforms of the Battersea girls easily outnumbered the hundred or so blue dresses of the Petersfield County High School girls. However, as the war progressed the numbers of local pupils gradually increased as boys and girls from outside the town came to live with relatives or friends in Petersfield in order to escape the bombing in other parts of the country. There was also a small number of Petersfield children who joined the visiting schools, Emanuel and Battersea Central, because there were vacancies on the school rolls.

(c) Portsmouth High School

Portsmouth High School for Girls was also evacuated during the war, the junior girls going to Hinton Ampner near Alresford, while the senior girls boarded at Adhurst St Mary in Sheet. This fine Victorian gothic mansion had been built for the Bonham-Carter family in 1858 and was currently occupied by Major and Mrs Alan Lubbock, who removed to the nursery quarters for the duration of the war. This was a particularly fortunate site for a school, not only because of the sumptuous house itself and the 600 acres of farmland and woodland all around, but it also had the blessing of Mrs Lubbock herself who had always been interested in education. She eventually became the Chairman of Governors of Petersfield Secondary Modern School and Petersfield Primary School. After the war part of the house was turned into four flats which Mrs Lubbock liked to let to members of the teaching profession. It goes without saying that the Portsmouth evacuees thoroughly appreciated their time there during the war years.

Adhurst St Mary today, unchanged since the war. (Author's Collection)

The Portsmouth High School girls who boarded at Adhurst throughout the war mostly remained until the age of eighteen, when they took their Higher School Certificate (A-Level equivalent); some of them then entered the Services and became Wrens (Women's Royal Naval Service, or WRNS), some chose to be nurses, some went (temporarily) into the Women's Land Army.

The interior of Adhurst St Mary was not unlike a hotel: the dormitories were upstairs where the servants' quarters would have been, the food was excellent, the library was used as a staff room, the ballroom was divided into two sections for different activities, Alan Lubbock's study became the senior girls' study, while the junior girls used the study which belonged to the Lubbocks' two sons. One classroom used was over the gun room in an outbuilding. For science subjects and library facilities, Churcher's College premises were used in the evenings. Mary Ray remembers being taught science at a bench at the back of a Churcher's laboratory, while Latin was being taught at the front of the class to Churcher's pupils. Bedales courts were borrowed for tennis practice and riding was available from Mr Grimshaw, the landlord of the Cricketers at Steep, whose daughters owned horses. For 2s 6d for an hour's riding, it was possible to go as far as Broadway's fields (now Broadway Park) where there were jumps. Gym and ballroom dancing were practised on the squash court when the weather was poor and outside on the front lawn when it was fine.

This was also where some of the Petersfield County High School girls took their Higher School Certificate. Here again, some unusual accommodation was pressed into educational service; one room, known as the Red Cross bathroom, where Matron held sway, doubled as a biology classroom. In all, about a hundred girls boarded in this building, most of them directly from Portsmouth, but also a few from Petersfield itself. Sports took place in the extensive grounds, but not without incident: before a lacrosse game could be played, cowpats had to be removed from the field and special rules adopted to cope with the inconvenience!

There were domestic duties for the girls too: they helped in the kitchens cutting bread and butter into individual ration sizes, for example, and the allotments in the grounds were worked to produce spring onions, radishes and carrots.

(d) Bedales School

At Bedales, some concern had been expressed by parents over the inadequacy of the school's arrangements for sheltering the children in the event of air raids; indeed, some children had already left, and this prompted the Chairman of the Governors, Mr G. Nelson Haden, to call for shelters to be dug in the school grounds. Several long trenches about 10ft deep were dug for the children just below 'Mrs Badley's Wood' in the top meadow; these were well-equipped affairs, with a roof, electric light, toilets, and bays with slatted wooden benches in them to accommodate separate groupings of about ten children. When the sirens sounded over Portsmouth at night-time everyone would get out of bed, wrap their red blankets around them and troop up through the vegetable gardens to the trenches. Sheila Trueman remembers this happening sometimes three times a night; Bedalians tend to be accustomed to lack of sleep, but these conditions exacerbated the normal boarding existence considerably.

The Bedalian ethos was, according to Paul Brown, somewhat curtailed during the war years – expeditions and adventurous activities were inevitably restricted and 'some of the old pioneering spirit which had once been a powerful flame was subdued and now only presented a faint glow'. However, by joining in some of the wartime activities in the district the pupils and staff made closer contact with the local community and thus, perhaps, dispelled some of the misunderstanding and even disapproval with which the school, especially in the earlier years, had been regarded.

The Headmaster who, in 1935, had immediately succeeded Bedales' founder, Mr Badley, was Mr F.A. Meier. The war years were to represent half of his tenure of office but, despite the butter rationing and blacked-out quad, the tin hats and gas masks, the extra hoeing and potato picking on free afternoons, the air-raid sirens and treks to the air-raid trenches at all hours of day and night, the ultimate desire to advance and develop in a Bedalian fashion was still very much alive.

(e) Primary Schoolchildren

Even the Senior Council School in St Peter's Road (the current Infants' School premises) was not immune from disruption. The large numbers of pupils which

Evacuees arriving at Petersfield station. (Author's Collection)

eventually filled the school premises, thanks to the presence of young Portsmouth evacuee children in the town, obliged the teaching to be carried out in two phases – local children attending for mornings one week and afternoons the next, alternating with the (junior) evacuee girls from Battersea who worked the other half of the day. Geoff Paddock remembers his mother being dissatisfied with this arrangement and he and his older brother were transferred to Steep School instead, until the arrangements at St Peter's Road were normalised. Shirley George remembers not having done much work there at the beginning of the war because the influx of Portsmouth children had the effect of closing the school for eight weeks at a time. Instead of going to classes, she and three others went into the school to peel potatoes and do other chores for the Portsmouth children who were temporarily housed in the Senior School. They even slept in the classroom until billets were found in town. At night the four pupils went round with the school caretaker and wished the newcomers 'good night'! With so many evacuees in the same premises the school was obliged to run a shift system and the Petersfield children's schooling was reduced to half-days.

THE FIRST TERM OF THE WAR

The logistical problem of housing the huge influx of schoolchildren in 1939 appeared, despite the potential for chaos, to have been managed reasonably satisfactorily.

During the first autumn term of the war, the schools, with their new regimes of dual accommodation and facilities which had threatened to disrupt the educational process, seemed in fact to have suffered only marginally. At the Churcher's College Presentation of Prizes ceremony in November 1939, which replaced the customary and more formal Speech Day, the Headmaster, Mr A.H.G. Hoggarth, mentioned the successful activities 'in which there is some life: the Scientific Society, the Music Club, the Debating Society, the Boys' Gardens, and Mr Ive's new potato plot'! He also expressed the wish that Captain Charles's annual trips to the continent – he had taken twenty-two boys to Paris the previous Easter – would not be interrupted for too long as they were a valuable contribution to the educational process. Wilson Atkinson started a Young Farmers' Club at the College, organising speakers, competitions, farm visits, camping at his father's farm in East Meon, helping with the harvesting, and arranging to look after calves, chosen from Herne Farm, at home. This was specifically aimed at introducing city boys to farming methods and practices. Herne Farm itself, run by Mr Noyce, covered the area of the present estate, and therefore provided wonderful walking country across the fields between, say, Heath Road and Ramshill – a fine and safe play area for children.

The shift system for the two boys' schools seemed to be working very successfully and relations between the two sets of pupils and teachers were excellent. Mr Hoggarth claimed that there was 'little serious loss from an educational point of view, especially if the extra hour and a quarter of leisure is used wisely'. At about the time of the 1938 crisis the War Office asserted that 'the Army Council consider it essential that the activities of the Junior Division of the Officers' Training Corps should continue with the least possible interruption in the event of war'. Churcher's attempted to fulfil this expectation and, despite the difficulties caused by the mobilisation of two of its staff, it endeavoured to carry on as normal.

Mount House, standing opposite Churcher's College (and since demolished and replaced by Pegswood House), had been bought by Mr Hoggarth to serve as an overflow for the boarders who until then had been housed at the top of the college building itself. It eventually became the boarding house for the whole college. Meanwhile, Churcher's Preparatory School occupied Heath Harrison House (next to Churcher's College) during the war and the boys were both taught and housed there, under Mr Jack Le Grice. (Heath Harrison, a relative of Leonard Cheshire, donated the house to Churcher's Headmasters but it was not until after the war that it was used by Mr Hoggarth's successor, Mr G.T. Schofield, for his family.) When the air-raid sirens went off during the war, the boarders would come down from their dormitories to sleep in the downstairs corridors in their sleeping bags.

The editor of *The Churcherian* (Churcher's College magazine) for December 1939 declared that the best way to cope with the war was to carry on with their own work in as normal a manner as possible. Two boys did in fact become 'Light-restriction Officers' and made temporary constructions and curtains for the blackout. Wilson Atkinson joined the AFS with a dozen other boys and undertook training on the use of water pumps in order to be prepared for any fires at the school.

Refugees from overseas also found a place in the Petersfield education system: at Bedales, where the international flavour always formed a part of its original philosophy anyway, there were Poles, Danes and Dutch pupils during the war, while at the Girls' High School a young Jewish refugee girl, Gretel Abrahamson, who had escaped Nazi-occupied Europe thanks to the *Kindertransport*, found a home in Harting and attended the school along with her English contemporaries.

In a quasi-poetic eulogy in the *Squeaker*, a Battersea teacher spoke of the warmth of Petersfield's welcome, the speed of the billeting process and the kind offers of help from all quarters. 'Working groups were organised and gradually routine school life, enriched by new experiences of the countryside and market square, became possible.' Emanuel School's historian, Roger Marjoribanks, wrote of this period:

> The burden of maintaining [the school's] morale naturally fell heavily on the staff; they now tended to see much more of their pupils in a pastoral role, establishing 'The Club' to provide some evening social life for the younger boys, and taking their holidays in rotation in order to ensure that boys always had some members of staff available.

As Christmas approached the government announced that it deprecated the return home of any evacuee children during the holiday period. In Petersfield entertainments were therefore organised in the new Town Hall, opened only three years previously, for the children from the Battersea and Emanuel Schools.

Mount House, the Churcher's College boarding house. (Author's Collection)

COUNCIL DELIBERATIONS

At their mid-September meeting the Petersfield Rural District Council discussed fire-fighting and evacuation issues, the payment of ARP workers, and food and fuel control (National Registration Day was fixed for 29 September). A sense of national emergency was clearly already in evidence, spreading from the State itself to individuals in their daily lives, as the ARP advert appearing in the *Squeaker* illustrated (see page 28).

By the end of October the ARP occupied various premises throughout the town, including certain rooms in the Town Hall, the library, St Peter's hall, the Scouts' headquarters, and Sheet Institute. The ARP organiser, Mr Caplen, was training new personnel and a siren had now been installed in Prince's Road. Initially the air-raid warning signal used in the town was that of the Amey brewery's siren in Frenchman's Road. If anything, Petersfield was over-prepared for any raids on the town which, ironically, had in any case been declared a 'safe area'.

At an Urban District Council meeting the same month the subject of evacuees was raised; there were a thousand billets in the town and householders received 10s 6d per week for the first child taken in and 8s 6d for each subsequent child. The evacuation scheme required many voluntary helpers and among these were two girls from Battersea Central School. The general supervision of all this necessary wartime effort, such as registration, the distribution of ration books, and the settlement of evacuees, had been carried out by the Clerk to the Council, Mr Percy Burley.

PETERSFIELD URBAN DISTRICT COUNCIL

The first meeting of the Petersfield UDC took place in 1895 at the old Town Hall which stood in front of St Peter's Church until 1898. The Council inherited a long tradition of local government in the town, the first Charter being granted by William, Earl of Gloucester, in the twelfth century. It is possible to trace the mayors of the old Borough of Petersfield from the fifteenth century.

In its early days the UDC assumed the functions of water supply, sewerage and refuse collection, street lighting, highways, the market, recreation grounds, and burials. In 1913 it purchased the manorial rights over the Heath and the market. The first Council houses were built at Noreuil Road in 1922 and residential development started to flourish. Regrettably, perhaps, some of the picturesque old street names became more prosaic: Nine Posts Lane, Cow Legs Lane and Golden Ball Street are now known respectively as Windsor Road, Station Road and Sussex Road.

In 1932 a boundary extension brought Sheet and Stroud within the District boundaries. The present Town Hall was built in 1935, partly from local rates and partly by public subscription. The last meeting of the UDC was held on 25 March 1974.

CHANGING TIMES

The influx of evacuees and the increasing movement of soldiers in and out of the town also had a social dimension: there was a need for recreational facilities within the town. The first of a series of dances to raise funds for the 'comfort' of troops was held at the Town Hall in November 1939, when the Petersfield Dance Orchestra provided many hours of music for the 150 people present. It was a time for morale-boosting among the population at large and an appeal under the heading 'Look after your airmen who look after you' appeared in the *Squeaker*. The 'Royal Air Force Comforts Fund' scheme, sponsored by the Air Ministry, gave an opportunity to people in all walks of life, young and old alike, to show in a practical way their appreciation and gratitude by providing cigarettes, tobacco, knitted wear, mouth organs, handkerchiefs, tins of sweets and chocolate, magazines and books, as well as games such as darts, shove-halfpenny boards and packs of cards.

The business community felt the hard times coming too. In an article in the *Squeaker* Petersfield's high-class tailor and outfitter, Edward Privett, called upon business people to show courage, confidence and patience in the commercial world, whose idealism and quality of standards had perhaps been rocked by some unscrupulous dealers.

Despite the necessary inconveniences, the restrictions and the adjustments to 'normal life' imposed by the wartime conditions now prevailing in Petersfield as elsewhere in the country, the town attempted to carry on its communal life as best it could. Indeed, many contemporary residents would have claimed that the town was relatively, even extraordinarily, unaffected by the worst impact the war was having in other areas, and this despite the proximity of Portsmouth and London. The town, with its influx of evacuated children and the additional numbers of elderly people from distant areas, was reported to be 'unusually full of life and movement', but the Indian summer of September 1939 had added to the feeling of normality, just as it provided the sensation of the 'phoney war' (as it was later referred to) during that autumn and winter. In fact, the apparent lack of any major military activity or threats led to the return home of a considerable number of the exiled London residents in Petersfield. Some people started going out after dark again, despite the warnings to stay at home and the reduction in transport facilities. The darkened streets had been deserted at night, but the re-opening of the local cinema (the Savoy in Swan Street) brought the townsfolk out again, despite the difficulty they had in finding their way home afterwards.

The desire on the part of the town to welcome its new guests in as friendly a manner as possible was clearly acknowledged by the local press, which spoke of the imported residents accommodating themselves well to the 'strange conditions and surroundings and manner of life' of the ordinary residents of the district. A considerable number of 'khaki-clad men' (as the *Squeaker* referred to them) frequenting the streets, homes and hostelries of the town carried home with them

The Taro Fair in the 1930s. (Author's Collection)

the good wishes and hospitality of Petersfielders with whom they came into contact. Patriotic programmes at the Savoy included such films as *Wings of the Navy* and *Air Devils*.

October brought the familiar Heath Fair (Taro Fair) to town and, although this year it was confined to a sale of horses and a few farming requisites, which disappointed many people, it did offer the feeling of stability and normality which everyone yearned for. It had been deemed unsuitable to hold a fun fair, yet several hundred people attended (fewer than the usual thousands in those days) and these were chiefly agricultural folk, dealers and gypsies and the like. Shirley George was lucky: she lived in Frenchman's Road at the time and the fair caravans were parked at the back of her house in the grounds of the Volunteer Arms (now Meon Close). She was invited to visit the caravans of the Romanies, where she was made most welcome. To add to the desire for normality that autumn, the Savoy cinema showed a Charlie Chan adventure, Boris Karloff in *Super Sleuth* and a romantic adventure *Sword of Honour*.

A committee was formed to arrange musical events in the town; this produced a concert for schools in December, when Handel's *Messiah* was performed under the baton of Dr Norman Newell of Emanuel School. Indeed, it was one of the first examples of the general contribution made by Emanuel School masters to the cultural and intellectual life of wartime Petersfield. For example, an Emanuel School history master, Mr J.W. Hunt, gave a well-received lecture on the current political situation in Europe and the Second Master, Stafford Hipkins, arranged for a West End cast to come and perform Goldsmith's *She Stoops to Conquer* in the Town Hall. There were numerous other social events in the town during this period; dances were held in the Town Hall, in Sheet village hall and in the Petersfield Working Men's Institute, and whist drives and rummage sales were held in other halls around the town.

It was a freezing Christmas period for the evacuees' first winter in the town – 35 degrees of frost had been recorded in one part of the country, the sea froze as it lapped the shore in West Sussex, and skating became possible in many parts of the country, including on the Heath Pond (to give it its correct name) in Petersfield. Peter Lyne describes that first winter as 'fearsome', but it didn't prevent him from cycling across the Pond! In the winter of 1939/40 there was a great freeze-up; a drizzle which had lasted about twenty-four hours froze as soon as it touched anything, so that everything was eventually covered in about three-quarters of an inch of ice – telephone wires stretched until they practically touched the ground and the Heath Pond was frozen over for weeks. Roy Maxwell remembers seeing a lady doing her shopping while skating along the High Street and pulling a sledge behind her; it became impossible to climb up the top end of Lavant Street to reach the station; the Emanuel OTC even drilled on the ice of the pond on skates!

The emergency services were operating actively by this time: the ARP, Red Cross, Fire Brigade, Special Constables and other voluntary bodies all contributed to the effort to keep the town safe and prepared for any untoward event. Even some

Skating on Heath Pond in the 1930s. (Mary Ray Collection)

private houses had been offered as schools or hospitals for evacuees in the event of an emergency. Parents and relatives of evacuees had already visited their children in the town and the fine weather had allowed everyone to enjoy hiking and excursions into the countryside. Arrangements had also been made for some form of indoor recreational activities for these people. In general, therefore, the town boasted a fine record for hospitality and friendliness from the outset; although some problems occurred with the reception of such quantities of people from many different parts of the south-east of England, these problems were debated at the Rural District Council (PRDC) meetings and usually resolved with alacrity.

Far from allowing evacuees to vent their frustration or their anxiety at their situation, however, many Petersfielders saw the natural fears hanging over the urban exiles as a potentially great opportunity for the town to show its sense of community, its determination to accommodate the newcomers and its willingness to share its pride in the rural environment. G. Frances Barnes, writing to the *Squeaker* from Bedales Lodge, wrote that the war had provided evacuation areas with a great opportunity to compensate for the insecurity and bewilderment of erstwhile city-dwelling children by offering them day nurseries which might eventually become nursery schools, 'which are the best education venture of the twentieth century'.

The removal of children from their parents in cities was far more than a change of environment, however, and nothing illustrates better the value of a rural upbringing than the experiment of the Camp Schools, set up under the Camps Act of 1939. In Petersfield, West Mark Camp School, which opened in 1940, provided just such an education. Nor did the social lives of the evacuated schoolchildren appear to suffer from the effects of the war: the Methodist church hall became an assembly hall for the girls of Battersea Central School in the mornings and a recreational venue for the Emanuel boys in the evenings, when it provided games, a library, and reading and writing facilities. The first real attempt to provide a proper social evening for the general community met with an almost embarrassing success when 250 people turned up. As time went by these 'Tuesday evenings at Station Road' became a feature of Petersfield's community life and there followed games evenings, singing, lantern lectures, debates, and musical and social evenings.

Phyllis White describes the Heath on fine days as 'an extraordinary sight, unbelievable to look back on, covered with swarms of children and young people. In some cases, whole families came down with their parents.' There were many animals grazing on the Heath in those days too, with the result that it was always well-cropped, and therefore ideal for the playing of ball games.

Some Petersfield High School girls joined a town 'Youth Squad' to pursue the war effort: they started an allotment in the garden of a house on Heath Road to raise funds for their enterprises, adopted a minesweeper and knitted garments for the sailors.

The first four months of the war had been something of a testing time for Petersfield: many hundreds of evacuated schoolchildren had had to be

A.R.P. CORNER

This week I invite Wardens to send in to the A.R.P. Office a report form (M1), reporting on the following incident. Report forms sent in will be corrected (if necessary) and returned to the Wardens who sent them. The name of the Warden should be written in the remarks portion of the form so that this can be done. Here is the imaginary incident :—

At 10 o'clock at night a German plane flies across the town and drops a stick of four large H.E. bombs, which in turn fall on the Senior Boys' School, The Bell Inn, William III Statue, and the Cinema. Fire breaks out in the Cinema, which is just closing, and a number of casualties are caused by splinter, and some are buried in the collapsed building, the bomb in the Square has fractured the H.T. cable which runs across. There is one casualty at the Bell Inn (the Inn was closed owing to shortage of beer), and a water-main burst near the School. There is a strong smell of gas at the Cinema. The Police are dealing with the casualty at the Bell Inn, and the G.P.O. Home Guard are already helping at the Cinema.

Wardens' Meeting, 7.30 p.m., Friday, 26th instant, at Town Hall.

THE ORGANISER.

Advert in the Hants and Sussex News, *1940. (Hampshire Museums Service)*

accommodated and billets found with people who, in some cases, had been unexpectedly called upon to help; the emergency and voluntary services had had to examine their procedures and adapt to the new conditions; all the schools had had to work hard to maintain a sense of normality in a reduced working day; and the town itself had had to retain its composure in the face of all these upheavals. The fact that so much of this transformation appeared to have succeeded – here, the 'phoney war' was a blessing – was a tribute to everyone in the town, not least to those in positions of responsibility. As if to underline and to symbolise the new living conditions, the weather had also changed, from the hot summer days of August to the first icy winter of the war four months later. It remained to be seen whether, when the war and its consequences began to be felt more keenly, the town's structures, its initial hospitality towards its guests, and the residents themselves could withstand the pressures they were likely to face.

CHAPTER TWO

1940

Petersfield Adjusts

EVACUATION

In April 1940 the Petersfield Urban District Council was informed that the town was to receive about 200–300 children from the Portsmouth area. In June some 150 boys and 100 girls arrived and were conveyed to the County School opened by Portsmouth Education Committee at West Mark Camp in Sheet. Their parents had opted to send them away from Portsmouth when the city suffered its first bombardment of the war. Coaches brought them from various schools in the Portsmouth area to West Mark Camp, situated just off the A272 behind Sheet Common. These were, to all intents and purposes, city day-school pupils who became boarders and were self-sufficient on their purpose-built site. Other Petersfield schoolchildren, and indeed a few adults, seem to have been totally oblivious to their presence in the area.

These were deemed to be 'delicate children and those likely to benefit from open-air life'. At the first anniversary celebrations of the opening of the West Mark Camp School a year later the Warden (Headmaster) Mr W.J. Hawkins praised the venture, thanks to which the Portsmouth children 'were spending their young lives in beautiful surroundings and under the most healthful and advantageous conditions'. It was the aim of this school to teach the children to consider others beside themselves, to work for the community, to be useful and self-reliant and to get to know something of country life. This educational experiment had, by the end of the war, evidently achieved its goals.

Judging by both the written reports and the spoken comments received from and about the evacuated children from the two London schools, they fared well on the whole: if any problems did occur the children were transferred as soon as possible to alternative billets. Dennis Geen talks of 'falling on his feet' in a house where he found a 'real foster mother'; he was not the only evacuee in the area to appreciate Petersfield to such an extent that he returned to settle in the town later in life. Evacuees talk of being treated like real sons and daughters when they were ill and of their parents being welcomed in the same billets when they came down from London for a weekend. Any boy from Emanuel who did not get on with his hosts could go to Lyndum House in the High Street, a sort of transit base from which, at best, questions of low morale could be discussed or, at worst, arrangements could be made to change billets. There was a constant need for such a centre, if only to alert the billeting authorities to individual problems or to act as an intermediary between the schools and the town's billeting officers. Naturally, if host couples or families had resented in any way having evacuees billeted on them in the first place

Lyndum House Hotel, High Street, during the war. (Petersfield Museum)

(there was an obligation for homes with space available to take them), relations could become strained. One example of such friction concerned an Emanuel boy who found himself billeted with a vegetarian family, which was something he was unaccustomed to in London; worse was the fact that he wasn't given a house key and, as both husband and wife were often out working in the evenings, he was obliged to wander the streets until they came back home. This situation continued for quite a while until one of his schoolmasters saw him in the town late one night; when the circumstances were explained, the boy was immediately relocated to another billet.

A report on evacuation in the Petersfield Rural District covering the first six months of the war produced by Sir Hugh Cocke, the organiser, revealed the following statistics: the number of unaccompanied children who had arrived on 1 September was 958, to which was added a small number already in the Reception areas who had been accepted for billeting, and a further number who joined their schools from London subsequently. This made a total of 1,075. This figure excludes Bramshott, an area reserved for military billeting.

The war on the home front, however, had become something of an anti-climax, if a welcome one. With the totally unexpected absence of any form of attack by the *Luftwaffe* on London the need for evacuation seemed to be over; already in the first few weeks of September there had been a trickle of evacuees returning from some areas to London and this soon became a small flood.

As a consequence, the number of unaccompanied children in billets in the Petersfield area had fallen to 718 by the end of February, a drop of 34 per cent. Seven months' experience of billeting had shown that the number of available and suitable billets had declined appreciably from the initial census figures, which had come to be regarded as over-optimistic. Nevertheless, after subtracting those householders who could not offer billets because of their age or infirmity, or because of their arduous war work and absence of domestic help, and a good number who had their own private evacuees, the balance of those who had not materially assisted with the billeting problem at all was quite small. Indeed, few districts could match the excellent arrangements for evacuees in Petersfield, thanks to the large and willing number of voluntary helpers, ably overseen first by Colonel Beazley and subsequently by Sir Hugh Cocke. Shirley George, who worked for Sir Hugh

Heath House, a convalescent home in the war, now demolished. (Petersfield Society)

for five years, found it both an interesting and a sad time: interesting because it was challenging and sad because the people who were being housed seemed disorientated; at the age of fifteen Shirley was already manning the phones at the Town Hall, answering queries about accommodation in the whole area covering the thirteen parishes they were responsible for, which stretched from Liss to Rowlands Castle.

In Sir Hugh Cocke's report, presented to the Rural District Council, mention was also made of the uniformly excellent health of children evacuated to the area. Three hospitals for evacuees had been established in requisitioned houses at Mooreys in Liss, The Yews in Horndean, and Heath House in Petersfield, the latter having been placed at the disposal of Emanuel School by its owners, Mildred and Gwendoline Russell. However, hospital admissions were few: there had been fifty-two admissions to Heath House out of a total number of eight hundred children in

Two members of the Domestic staff at West Mark Camp School. (Author's Collection)

the urban district area. These children may have been injured or orphaned by the Portsmouth bombing raids. Regrettably, Heath House, a fine eighteenth-century building, became derelict after the war and was pulled down in the late 1950s. Some of the original outbuildings still stand, however, together with the railings and gateway chains.

WEST MARK CAMP SCHOOL

Sir John Anderson's 'Committee on Evacuation', established by the Home Secretary in 1938, proposed the construction of many hundreds of camp schools in rural areas, originally conceived as centres where children from large cities could go and experience life in a country environment for a term. At the outbreak of war, however, only about thirty of these had been completed and they started to be used by local authorities as permanent boarding schools for evacuated children of secondary age. The newly formed Petersfield Air Training Corps (1927 Squadron) used the site for training purposes and the Camp Manager, Mr J. Burke, an ex-Regimental Sergeant Major, became its Commanding Officer.

Portsmouth, being a prime target area, took up the offer by the local education authority which had leased West Mark Camp from the National Camps Corporation.

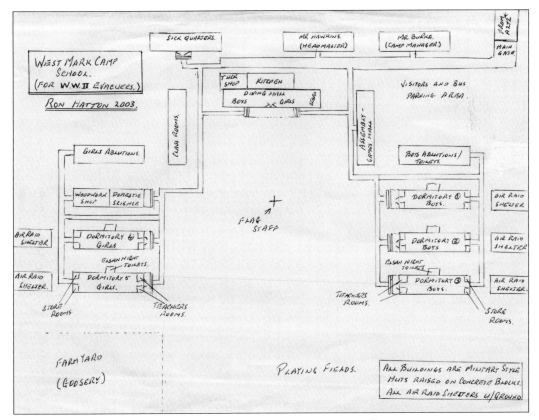

Sketch plan of West Mark Camp, drawn by Ron Hatton. (Author's Collection)

Situated on a 7-acre site adjacent to the A272 and near Sheet Common, West Mark Camp School was to become the home to many Portsmouth evacuees between 1940 and 1945, the first 250 of which arrived in a convoy of green and cream Southdown buses on 24 June 1940. In one week, under the direction of Head-master Mr W.J. Hawkins and the Camp Manager, the dormitories were furnished, classrooms set up, the dining hall, kitchens and hospital equipped, and catering and medical supplies brought in.

Toni Leighton's anniversary reminiscence describes the site of the camp, now demolished: the wooden buildings were raised off the ground and set roughly on three sides of a square. Across the top of the square was the dining hall, boys sitting at one end, girls at the other. Boys and girls were taught separately in one block of four classrooms, and five dormitories, two for girls and three for boys, stood behind the classrooms. In the centre of the site was a large grassed area, with a tall flagpole in the centre, which was the children's playground and meeting area. A small hospital block, ablution blocks and an assembly hall completed the general camp facilities, other smaller huts and bungalows being used by the teaching and domestic staff.

An almost military-style routine ensured the discipline and well-being of the children, but naturally required some adjustment on their part too. Their lives were governed by the groups of eight into which they were formed – whether it was in the dormitories, dining room or classrooms. This number was critical for the rapid and safe removal of the children to the shelters in the event of air-raid alerts. Far from being a straitjacket, however, the routine served them well and created a just society: each of the six dormitories had to produce a camp concert once every six weeks and some of the fondest memories of former pupils are of those concerts. Ron Hatton can still recite and sing his favourite: *The Pigcamelephantelopeacoctopussycow*, a West Mark Camp showstopper which he has since taught to his children and his grandchildren! Indeed, it is quite self-evident that the regular concerts were the highlight of the children's existence, a means of forgetting the war outside the camp, but, even more important from an educational point of view, a solid foundation for the unity of spirit and purpose so necessary for those children at that difficult period of their lives. Josephine Gillmore, who was the longest serving pupil at West Mark (from 1940 until 1945), remembers the whole atmosphere there as exciting and fun. She talks of the wonderful meals, the annual Sports Days, when parents would come up from Portsmouth by train or a specially hired bus, the country and Scottish dancing for girls (the boys did sports at these times), the free Saturdays when the pupils could get a pass to go into Petersfield to the Savoy cinema or to shop in Woolworths, the Christmas parties and the various girls' sports of which Josephine became captain. But it was the village of Sheet which she holds most fondly in her memories: it was there that she attended confirmation classes at St Mary's church, there that the children reached after crossing the 'ravine' on Sheet Common and wading through the River Rother, there that she and her hungry friends bought a bag of scones from the side door of the Harlequin café, which stood next to the Half Moon in Sheet in those days. Her memories of that period are gastronomic: of the two pennyworth of carrots the children bought in Sheet village, the chestnuts they harvested in Durford Wood, the mushrooms they picked for their teachers in the top field behind West Mark, or even the potatoes they lifted, which they would peel and eat raw.

The transition for both the teachers, who found themselves working a 24-hour day, and the pupils, who made the change from town to country life sometimes only with difficulty, was a shock, but one which eventually brought positive responses from the whole community. Runaways were nearly always recovered before they had travelled very far – and often promptly returned to West Mark by their parents! One homesick (and anonymous) boy's ingenuity took him and some friends by goods train from Petersfield station sidings to Fratton goods yard one Friday night. The boys had crawled under the tarpaulin covering the goods wagon, waited until the early hours of the morning when the train left, and eventually arrived in Fratton goods yard; then they just needed to jump over a fence and run to Milton where they lived. On arrival there a police car and an irate father met them, they were bundled into the police car and taken back to West Mark, where they got the cane!

Raymond Hatton
D3
West Mark Camp
Sheet, Nr.
Petersfield
18/3/41

Dear Grandma,

I hope you are all right and Auntie Elsie. I hope you have sent me the ink and other things. Could you send me some coppers, and some darning wool and needles, and my sheath knife. I want brown and grey wool and a looking glass. I wish you would write to me. Last night we had a siren, and plenty of guns and planes. I do not like it very much up hear. On Tuesday, Friday, Saturday and Sunday we are allowed out of the camp. On Tuesday I went to Sheet and I bought a bottle of orange crush 5½d. The visiting times are 2 o'clock on Sunday, and if you come up or Dad comes up I will be able to come out with you or Dad. At night we have a story before the lights are put out. We have breakfast at 8 o'clock then school then dinner, then we have the afternoon off, then tea at 4.0, then at 5.15 we have school till 7.0, then we have supper and then bed. So good bye for now.

Raymond

P.S. Can I have a real of cotton as well. Don't forget to write to me. And ask Barbara to write to me.

Raymond Hatton's letter to his parents in Milton, 18 March 1941. He was at West Mark Camp for eigthteen months.

On Saturdays the children were allowed to go into Petersfield where they went to the Saturday morning picture show at the Savoy cinema, browsed round Woolworths or bought cakes and sweets in the small shops. Sunday was a relaxing day and a time for families to visit the camp once a month. Children from Catholic families attended Mass at St Laurence's church in Petersfield, while the rest walked in crocodile to St Mary Magdalene, Sheet, for morning service.

The war was never completely absent for the West Mark Camp community, however, and the devastating Portsmouth blitz of January 1941 could even be seen from the camp (in the gap between Butser and Wardown hills); the children must have been worried about the fate of their parents.

A very popular form of entertainment was the evening sing-song at which Mr or Mrs Hawkins would play the piano and lead the singing, including the camp song:

> There is a happy place down West Mark way
> Where we get bread and jam four times a day
> Eggs and bacon we don't see
> We get no sugar in our tea
> And we are gradually fading away, fading away!

Mr Hawkins, whose forte was music and who is described by Ron Hatton as 'a real gentleman', had an amusing party piece which consisted of sitting at the piano, taking off his shoes and socks, swinging back on his chair and playing the piano with his toes!

With memories of homespun concerts, the appreciation and love of the idyllic natural surroundings, the variety and excitement of new experiences and challenges, it is hardly surprising that most ex-West Mark pupils regard those years as the happiest of their lives. For 'townies' it represented an insight into another lifestyle, one which taught the children to understand and respect country life, the trees, plants and animals of the region.

After the war ended West Mark continued to be used as a camp school until the mid-1950s, and, briefly, to house refugees. Since then, all traces of the camp have disappeared and two houses now stand on the site behind the Midhurst Road.

INTERIM ASSESSMENT OF THE EVACUATION

By the end of July it was possible to assess the progress of the evacuated schoolchildren in Petersfield during their first full academic year away from home. Instead of a Speech Day at Adhurst St Mary, 'At Homes' were arranged to give an opportunity to parents of Portsmouth High School girls to see how school life was flourishing under the changed conditions. The Headmistress, Miss G.E. Watt, reported that the experiment in communal life was full of interests: girls and staff alike took a share of the domestic duties; they also shared activities within the school clubs, which now had even greater scope as the daily journeys to and from school had been eliminated. Students had learnt many valuable lessons in good neighbourliness, while those with a practical bent had found the recognition denied to them in a day school. Only children found companionship, not just in work but also in recreation. Most girls had learnt to accept without question their share of the uncongenial jobs.

At the Emanuel School Speech Day in the Town Hall the same month, the Headmaster, Mr C.G.M. Broom, spoke of the odyssey embarked on by the contingent of roughly 450 boys the previous September, whose lives in Petersfield had not merely been maintained but enriched by the experience. He considered the pupils to have been peculiarly lucky in their new country environment, rich in varied beauties and interests and in the hospitable reception they had found with foster parents. What he called 'the daily Box and Cox tenancy' with Churcher's had enabled the schools to learn much from each other and in such circumstances, he claimed, it was not surprising that the past year had been as successful as any good year in normal conditions. Their programme of activities had actually extended beyond their pre-war limits, the novelties including the introduction of fencing, a stable converted for use as a metalwork shop, and the necessary organisation in the winter of a clubroom for indoor activities in which a cinema had been invaluable. An allotment at Sheet, which the Urban District Council had put at their disposal, was now yielding a valuable crop and, in order to assist local farmers, a group of senior boys was going to camp in the vicinity in August. The music department, under Dr Newell, had flourished and given ready support to local concerts and choral performances.

The boys, now fully fledged members of a boarding school, were enjoying more freedom and more opportunity of seeing their parents than boarders usually did. Their conditions of exile from London had made them more self-reliant; they had shown resourcefulness and adaptability, enjoyed the many pleasures and advantages of country life and, in particular, the skating, fishing and boating available on the Pond.

Not all the exiled Londoners survived their new rural existence, however, and families occasionally returned to the capital after only a few days here. Peter Winscom had received a family from London at Stroud Farm in 1939 – a lady, her three children and her mother – who seemed sad and wholly disorientated. They spent their time walking into Petersfield to watch the trains go by! They soon returned home. One of Gladys Turner's evacuees from London complained that she never got given fish and chips and buns, but only fresh vegetables from the garden! A small five-year-old boy from a poor area of London was evacuated to April Austin's house early on in the war – 'a grubby little boy, but he looked like an angel' – and her mother decided 'Tommy' badly needed a bath. But Tommy decided otherwise and screamed his head off. Despite this, Mrs Austin managed to bath him (with a few drops of Dettol in the bath!) and lay a meal at the dining-room table for all of them. Tommy, however, didn't seem to understand the concept of mealtimes and just sat in the doorway, watching the people going by, something he was obviously used to in London. Eventually, however, Tommy adapted to country life and remained in Sheet, with another family, for the rest of the war.

Portsmouth families seemed to cope better with the conditions in the area; whether this was because they had no alternative as their houses had been badly damaged or demolished by the severe bombing at home, or whether they were more aware of the demands and strictures of country life, it is hard to say, but several hundred evacuees settled in Petersfield for the duration of the war. At Adhurst Farm, for example, the Groves firm of solicitors took over the sitting room, and a bedroom in the house was occupied by a dockyard family of four.

EDUCATION

The deprivations of the war did not unduly affect the education of either the Petersfield children or the evacuees who were to share their accommodation and facilities for so many years. On congratulating an Emanuel pupil on gaining an Exhibition in Modern Languages at St Catherine's College, Cambridge, the *Squeaker* concluded that such achievements established conclusively that, far from evacuation having proved deleterious to the work of the pupils, it had actually contributed in no small measure to it. The conclusion drawn here was that, whereas in London the Emanuel pupils were scattered over a very wide area, in Petersfield the boys and staff were always within easy reach of one another and this accessibility had enabled Sixth Form masters in particular to give far more individual attention to their pupils than would have been possible in normal circumstances. An equally warm tribute was clearly also being paid here to the Petersfield 'host mothers', who gave the evacuees the privacy and quiet indispensable to their work in these difficult times. The success of the evacuation for Emanuel schoolboys can be measured by the fact that after seven months of wartime the drift back to London had only taken away twenty of the 444 boys who had come down from London the previous autumn. Even their parents had admitted that the boys were bored during the holidays in London and were looking forward to returning to Petersfield to the new life which they had established for themselves.

It would not be contentious to say that, for their part, the Emanuel boys' presence in Petersfield also contributed to the town's social and intellectual life, and the town's traders naturally welcomed the influx of spending power, albeit relatively limited, which they represented.

At Churcher's Presentation of Prizes in December, which replaced the more formal Speech Days of peacetime, the Headmaster, Mr Hoggarth, spoke of the usefulness of the farming work performed by some boys in the school, both with individual farmers and at the farming camp organised at Long Sutton; some pupils had also been helping with hop-picking at Bentley. In the school grounds there was an allotment to the east of the swimming pool, where a fair crop of potatoes was lifted under the direction of Mr Ive, while some tree-felling was organised by Mr Turner. As far as the war effort was concerned, some boys had participated in signalling and first-aid classes, while others had helped the air-raid wardens as watchers or spotters, fire-fighters or light-restriction officers.

While the boys of Emanuel School were billeted in private houses around the town, the senior girls of Portsmouth High School were accommodated and taught at Adhurst St Mary, which housed about a hundred Sixth Form girls throughout the war. Although Miss Watt was the titular Head of the school, she put herself in charge of the junior girls at Hinton Ampner, while Miss Thorn, an English mistress, took control of the Adhurst section of the school. Not all the educational facilities required were available to any one school, and this inevitably necessitated a good deal of sharing (and travelling) by large numbers of pupils and their teachers to and from the various educational establishments in Petersfield.

At the Petersfield Girls' County High School Speech Day that December, the Headmistress, Miss Dorothy Chadwick, spoke in an upbeat fashion: she was gratified that her determination to hold a Speech Day had been justified by the presence of a large number of parents and friends (they had had to cancel the event the previous year); she felt that, had the school not had to share its premises, they would not have discovered the resourcefulness of the Governors in finding supplementary accommodation (often better than the existing school building!); she was delighted by what had been achieved in the past year, despite the cramped conditions which had curtailed some normal activities; finally, she was able to announce an increase in the size of Form VI, which showed that wise parents had encouraged their daughters to fit themselves for the world of work which they could enjoy both in peace and war.

The Headmistress of Battersea Central School for Girls, Dr B. Hall, wrote to the Petersfield Urban District Council thanking the town for the 'exceedingly efficient and kindly manner in which the billeting of their new entrant pupils had been carried out'. She continued: 'Petersfield would indeed be a pleasant memory for many of them in years to come.' Dr Hall was herself billeted with the Headmistress of Sheet School, Mrs Bennetts. Sheet School received some evacuee children and teachers from both London and Portsmouth schools.

The following year Dr Hall's successor, Miss K. Cocksedge, likewise publicly thanked the town for the way in which it had looked after the Battersea girls for nearly two years, enabling the school to continue to function practically full-time. She made a special plea for the girls to remain in Petersfield for three weeks during the summer holidays rather than be sent back to the danger areas. To relieve the foster parents of this burden Hylton House (later to become Moreton House) would be kept open both mornings and afternoons during that time. Interestingly, it was Miss Cocksedge who, after two years of the war had elapsed, declared at a Petersfield Girls' High School Speech Day that 'In some ways, schooling for girls was easier in wartime than during peace, since girls, now so often reminded how valuable their services were and what interesting work awaited them, felt that they could help in public and industrial life.' It was, of course, such a realisation throughout the nation at this time that led to the far greater employment of women in many new occupations after the war.

SIR REGINALD DORMAN-SMITH

The Member of Parliament for Petersfield at this time was Sir Reginald Dorman-Smith, who served as Minister for Agriculture and Fisheries in Neville Chamberlain's National government until the Coalition government of Winston Churchill took over the running of the country in May 1940.

His appeals to farmers in September and October 1939 will be remembered for one phrase in particular:

> Half a million more allotments properly worked will provide potatoes and vegetables that will feed another million adults and one and a half million children for eight months out of twelve ... So, let's get going. Let 'Dig for Victory' be the motto of everyone with a garden and of every able-bodied man and woman capable of digging an allotment in their spare time.

As everywhere in the country, Petersfielders took the exhortation seriously and soon bean sticks and rows of cabbages began to appear in both front and back gardens.

At a public meeting held at the Festival Hall in support of the special wartime National Savings Campaign in December 1939, Sir Reginald gave a review of wartime problems, concentrating on the need for self-imposed rationing: 'The voluntary discipline of a free people is an unbeatable force', he said, and stated that the government was relying on Britons to exercise the utmost economy, preferably by rationing themselves, rather than the government having recourse to the law to impose rationing.

Sir Reginald was appointed Governor of Burma in December 1940. Shortly afterwards, however, owing to restrictions on the extent of civil administration in Burma, he returned to Britain in 1941. He was appointed Vice-President of the National Farmers' Union in January 1942 but found himself moved again by the British government, this time to India in May 1942. He became Governor of Burma once more at the end of the war.

ENTERTAINMENTS

The Petersfield Musical Festival, founded in 1901, had not taken place during the whole of the First World War. However, thanks to sheer perseverance and enthusiasm, it did continue throughout the Second World War (with the sole exception of 1944), albeit in a reduced format, and without all of the customary competitions for choirs. The conductor, Adrian Boult, who had been knighted in 1937, the year of the coronation of King George VI, continued to inspire all participants at the Festival. Although there were only two days of performances in 1940, the presence of evacuated children in Petersfield allowed for a Children's Day, with choirs from Battersea Central School, Emanuel School and Portsmouth High School, together with Petersfield High School, Bramshott Boys and Blendworth Junior.

Various problems for the Musical Festival occurred during the war: the Town Hall served as the main base for the ARP; there was no raised platform for the choirs to use; the blackout and the absence of late-night buses deterred some people from attending; finally, with so many people, especially women, involved in fire-watch duties or caring for evacuees, there were fewer and fewer singers in the choirs.

For the soldiers and evacuees who found themselves in Petersfield during the first Christmas of the war, there were entertainments provided: a large gathering of soldiers and civilians were given a cheery concert at the YMCA, with a baritone soloist and an elocutionist providing the main attractions, and community singing afterwards. A New Year's carnival dance was held at the Town Hall which attracted well over 300 people, while about 150 evacuee children were taken to the Savoy cinema to see the Shirley Temple film *Little Princess*, before being given a tea party at the Town Hall, with Christmas tree, crackers and boisterous games! The post office recorded a number of postings of Christmas cards and parcels 'quite up to average'.

Unbeknown to their teachers, the evacuated boys and girls from the two Battersea schools occasionally went to the Savoy together. One of the most popular films of the whole war period was shown in April 1940: this was *Goodbye, Mr Chips*, with Robert Donat starring as the eponymous hero.

School outings to the Savoy were also arranged, and after seeing the film of Gilbert and Sullivan's *The Mikado* some of the girls became fans of the music – and still are! Roy Barrow often went to the Savoy with his parents on a Sunday afternoon; he recalls how the smoke was so thick inside that he used to throw orange peel up in the air so that it would be illuminated in the light from the projector!

CANTEENS

Food was regularly being supplied in the various voluntary canteens in the town. During Christmas and New Year 1939–40 over five hundred men were served cooked meals at the Winton House canteen in the High Street, while at the Petersfield Public Institution (generally known as the workhouse), at the bottom of Ramshill, the ninety inmates received a generous Christmas lunch consisting of roast rabbit or pork, beef or mutton, parsnips, Brussels sprouts, potatoes, plum pudding, beer and light drinks, followed by a packet of desserts (nuts, sweets and chocolates). Mr Ixer, the warden, remarked that, despite the war, they had fared as well as they had done in other years. The diet for the Institution's inmates in 1940 was said to be healthy and wholesome and looked much the same as the diet for the general public at that time. Tramps could find a night's rest and a meal at the workhouse at any time, provided they did a day's work such as cutting wood or bringing in the coal.

The inauguration of the British Legion canteen, which began functioning in St Peter's church hall in January 1940, ensured that even more men and women in the Services were catered for – approximately two hundred hot meals were served there on Saturday 13 January 1940 alone. Run almost entirely by ladies, it offered meals on four evenings a week, from Thursday to Sunday, and had a small billiard table and a darts board for recreation as well. During the war many hundreds of service people were to enjoy the facilities available in this canteen and rest centre.

Captain C.H.L. Woodhouse. (Author's Collection)

CAPTAIN C.H.L. WOODHOUSE AND HMS *AJAX*

Petersfield was directly associated with the first real sea battle of the war, which was waged on 13 December 1939. That winter, many attacks by U-boats on merchant shipping had begun in the North Atlantic. In the South Atlantic, beyond the operational reach of the U-boats, Allied shipping was being harassed by surface raiders of which the pocket battleship Admiral Graf Spee was one. A group of Royal Navy cruisers had been tracking the *Graf Spee* for some time and, after inflicting considerable damage to it, had forced it to seek refuge in the neutral Uruguayan port of Montevideo on the River Plate. International law allowed the Uruguayan authorities to refuse to harbour a seaworthy vessel and the German Captain, Captain Langsdorff, was given the choice of surrendering or putting to sea again. The latter course was chosen by the humiliated Captain, who subsequently scuttled his ship, then committed suicide.

It had been a brilliant and resounding strategic victory for the three British cruisers involved,

the *Ajax*, *Achilles*, and *Exeter*. Of these, the *Ajax* was commanded by Captain C.H.L. Woodhouse, whose family lived in Weston Road, Petersfield. Captain Woodhouse's wife Barbara was the younger daughter of Dr H.M. Brownfield, a much respected resident of the town whose surgery had been in the Old College in College Street. Two ironic coincidences which the Battle of the River Plate recalled were, firstly, that Captain Woodhouse's distinguished naval career had begun in the First World War when, as a lieutenant on HMS *Bristol*, he had already been involved in action against the Admiral Graf Spee in the Battle of the Falkland Islands in 1914, and, secondly, that the hero of this action, Admiral Sir Doveton Sturdee, had also been a Petersfield resident.

As a result of the gallant and daring pursuit of, and eventual victory over, the *Graf Spee*, Captain Woodhouse was awarded the CB (Companion of the Bath) and he was decorated by King George VI on 2 February 1940.

HMS Ajax. *(Royal Naval Museum, Portsmouth)*

FOOD SUPPLIES

The *Graf Spee* episode of December 1939 was seized upon as a timely tonic and a useful tool for propaganda. The name became a byword for battles to be won: even farmers were exhorted to win the '*Graf Spee* battle of production' to increase the provision of foodstuffs for the nation, as a government advertisement showed.

Needless to say, rural areas fared better for food during the war and many Petersfielders remember provisions of meat, milk and eggs being generally available, even if not in great quantities. David Martin, whose grandfather was a gamekeeper, remembers eating rabbits and pigeons. Fruit and vegetables were also in reasonably good supply, either provided by friends or colleagues who lived in the outlying villages, or willingly grown by many people in their town gardens following the precepts of the 'Dig for Victory' campaign. So successful was this campaign that there was little call for allotments in Petersfield.

A sophisticated networking system ensured that word spread of a special delivery – 'they've got bananas at the shop' – and children would be on their bikes to go and collect the latest delicacy.

Everybody had their own contacts for food supplies: Mary Ray remembers eating cobnuts given to her father by Mr Seward at Weston Farm; Ted Baigent looked after a large garden with potatoes, broad beans, runner beans, gooseberries, red- and blackcurrants – Sheet has a particularly good sandy, loamy soil for such produce. On the numerous farms around Petersfield at the time there was a plentiful supply of rabbits, pigeons, chickens and bread, some of which could be obtained by almost anyone in the town itself. However, for anyone who kept chickens, and there were many families in Petersfield who did, the normal egg ration had to be curtailed.

Food parcels would occasionally arrive from South Africa, consisting of dried and glacé fruits – pure luxury! The real delight came later in the war, however, when tinned Spam and baked beans became available for the first time, supplementing the occasional rabbit or chicken from farms or back gardens and the fresh vegetables which people grew on their allotments. Surprisingly, bread was freely available during the war and it wasn't until 1946 that a nationwide shortage caused it to be rationed. By then, grain from Britain was being exported to Eastern Europe and Russia.

Cooking became more inventive: Geoff Paddock's mother made dandelion wine; many families made cakes with dried egg powder; Norma Collins's mother made a concoction referred to as 'kettle broth' which consisted of bread, pepper and salt, butter and hot water! The Mackarness family, down on their uppers during the worst of the rationing period, ate 'ropot', roast (meat) paste on toast! In the Burleys's vegetable garden glitter strips were hung up to ward off the birds – this worried their neighbour who thought the glinting would attract German bombers. The *Squeaker* carried an article encouraging people to keep bees in order to supplement their sugar ration.

Some meals were truly unpalatable – Jenny Dandridge remembers eating nettles as vegetables, and some school meals were so indigestible that she feigned illness to escape the hardship of lunchtimes at Bedales. However, on the whole, children were

PLOUGH NOW !

by day...

and night...

...AND BEAT THE WEATHER !

Farmers! By ploughing now you can win the equivalent of a mighty naval battle! By providing food for the nation and by making your farms self-contained and independent of overseas feeding stuffs, you make both our shipping and our money available for buying munitions from abroad.

Win your Graf Spee battle of production by ploughing up now!

Farmers! Plough now by day and night.
Play your part in the fight for right.

★TO FARMERS AND WORKERS

The Prime Minister, speaking on February 28th :

" The Minister of Agriculture made a pronouncement last December, when he said : 'If the increase in home production that we want is to be obtained, then the prices must be such as would give a reasonable return to the farmer and enable the farmer to pay a fair wage to the worker.' I want to say again that the War Cabinet endorse that declaration by the Minister of Agriculture."

Advert in the Hants *and Sussex News, 1940. (Hampshire Museums Service)* relatively well fed in the schools: at the Girls' High School April Austin remembers eating plenty of mutton stew (often with fatty globules floating in it); she also ate something mysterious called 'railway pudding'.

Notices appearing in the press indicate that at this early stage of the war food was not in particularly short supply. There was some reduction in the range of teas available and butter was not plentiful; however, meat production and supply were not yet controlled, and the adoption of a standard quality of margarine had promoted its rapid production and distribution to make up for the shortfall in butter.

Scarcity breeds a black market, but it may also stimulate enterprise. Emanuel pupils remember with affection their comrade (who shall remain nameless), who was clearly a born entrepreneur: as school lessons started at 1.30 p.m. and did not finish until 5.30 p.m., with only a ten-minute break in mid-afternoon, the boys naturally became hungry. Our budding entrepreneur did a deal with the Co-op, who provided him with several dozen rolls per day and, paying some acolytes to help, he filled these with Marmite or jam and sold them during breaktime. This fast became quite a lucrative business, so much so that the Headmaster complimented him upon his enterprise – but at the same time insisted that some of the profits go to the school! That boy, need it be said, became a captain of industry in later life! The capitalist did not get away entirely scot-free at school, however; he had to endure (and no doubt relish) confrontations with a rabidly Socialist English master, who challenged him to public debate on the principles and morality of economic theory!

DIFFICULTIES OF LIFE IN PETERSFIELD

It would of course be misleading to argue that all was rosy in the life of Petersfielders at this time. A twelve-year-old schoolboy was found guilty at Petersfield Juvenile Court of twice stealing bicycles in the town; he was bound over for twelve months, fined the sum of £2 and warned to be of good behaviour in future. However, by far the most numerous offences committed in these early war years related to the failure to adhere to the regulations concerning the blackout, the inadequacy of car or bicycle headlight masking, or the showing of even a fraction of light from a house window. At Petersfield Petty Sessions in May and June 1940, for instance, heavy fines were imposed for these offences, as well as for the theft of petrol, for speeding and for the failure to license a vehicle. Nor was it sufficient to ride bicycles without lamps in order to remain invisible – this was also an offence and a fine was imposed.

ARP wardens patrolled the town regularly and were empowered to prosecute any householder who failed, however slightly, to obey the blackout regulations. These wardens were also responsible for other duties in the town; Shirley George, despite being too young for the kind of work involved, joined the ARP and spent some nights on duty on the roof of the Old College where she worked for the Rural District Council.

The following October, two entertainments in aid of the Spitfire Fund took place at the Town Hall: a feast of inspiring music devised by Kathleen Merritt and the performance of four plays in the evenings. As during all of the many fund-raising events in town during the war, it was Churcher's College OTC Band which would provide musical publicity and march up and down the High Street to drum up support. In a lighter vein, the Savoy was that summer showing *Nurse Edith Cavell*, starring Anna Neagle, and *Charley's Aunt*, with Arthur Askey in the title role.

The Heath Fair that year consisted solely of an auction sale of horses; there was a complete absence of any public amusements.

As the number of troops passing through the town was increasing significantly, it became clear that more restaurant facilities were urgently needed. The Drill Hall canteen in Dragon Street provided catering and recreational facilities for a large number of troops (about three thousand meals were served in the course of an average week). There was also a library and a mending circle, and hundreds of letters were sent from there using the writing materials provided. Volunteers also organised dances three nights a week in the hall. When evacuees started arriving in Petersfield after the first terrible raids on Portsmouth, it was in the Drill Hall that they were fed under the guidance of the indefatigable Mrs Kathleen Money-Chappelle.

The same hall was also the venue for the manufacture of camouflage netting later in the war, a heavy and thankless task which involved getting dyed with the colours of the materials used.

A less arduous but no less appreciated activity was performed by naval wives, who had simply moved with their families to Petersfield to be near their husbands based at Portsmouth. They worked for the Naval War Libraries whose job was to rebind books to send off to ships at sea; one lady who did this work was the wife of Captain Woodhouse of HMS *Ajax* fame.

The following month some 250 people took part in an evening of community hymn-singing in the Town Hall, including quite a number of men from the Armed Forces. This concert was to have been broadcast by the BBC, but the telephone lines were down that evening, which made this impossible.

PROGRESS OF THE WAR

At the beginning of the war any warning of an impending air-raid in Petersfield came from the hooter on the premises of the Itshide rubber factory which was at the top of Sandringham Road, the site now occupied by Balmoral Way. Later, a siren was mounted on a tower beside the Town Hall and another was situated in The Avenue, where a fire engine was also stationed. Messages about impending raids came from the Observer Corps on the top of Butser Hill, which were then relayed to the Town Hall where the siren was switched on. Those on duty then had to telephone to the ARP stations, the fire station, the police station and the hospitals. Certain buildings, like the Itshide factory and the gasworks off Hylton

Appealing for funds for Warship Week, 1942. (Petersfield Society)

Road (now part of Tesco's car park), were the first to receive warnings. The control centre for the ARP was located at the Town Hall where, in 1939, the ceilings had been reinforced and the exterior sandbagged. A public air-raid shelter had also been built in front of St Peter's church. One of Clive Ellis's duties, as an engineering surveyor to the Urban District Council, was to inspect cellars in private houses to see whether they could be reinforced and turned into air-raid shelters. During air-raid warnings at Petersfield County High School the girls sheltered in the school cellar.

In May 1940 the evacuation from Dunkirk saw a third of a million troops cross from the continent back into Britain. Thanks in part to the inspirational, rallying speeches of Churchill at that time, however, it was far from being perceived as the humiliating defeat it might have become in the public view, and instead represented an upsurge of morale for the home nation, who were able to give their full support to the returning regiments. In Sheet, for example, as the troops returned up the London Road to their bases in Surrey and London, Mrs Todd provided sustenance at her Harlequin café, situated next to the Half Moon pub.

There were several mobile anti-aircraft (ack-ack) batteries in Petersfield, one of which was stationed at the top of Tilmore Road (now Kimbers) and which made Geoff Paddock's house in Heathfield Road shake. On Tilmore bridge, metal posts were sunk into the road to prevent tanks crossing. Another mobile battery patrolled up and down London Road in Sheet during the Battle of Britain in the summer of 1940.

Throughout that summer many people witnessed the dogfights taking place in the skies over the district: Ted Baigent remembers seeing two British aircraft being shot down in the Milland Valley, and a Messerschmitt 109 which, after it had been shot, rose up in the sky, stalled, then plummeted down at Ditcham. Charles Sammonds witnessed a Bristol Blenheim crashing in Liss Forest with a huge explosion from some of the ammunition it still had on board. Geoff Paddock saw a returning Spitfire on fire and plunging downwards – the pilot baled out too low but landed near the old vicarage in Steep, while his plane came down in Harrow Lane. Steve Pibworth remembers a land mine being dropped on Butser Hill, and the enormous crater it caused. As was always the case with such incidents, groups of schoolboys would immediately leap on to their bikes and race to see what they could find at the crash site – equally promptly they would be turned back by any officials already there, who were probably as anxious to defend the military interest as they were to prevent young eyes from seeing any carnage. With hindsight, it seems a ghoulish activity on the part of the boys, but they did it more out of curiosity than morbidity and it can be explained by their excitement at the real military activity they found on their doorstep. Looting for souvenirs was a commonplace activity and there are many people today who still treasure their 'finds' from this period. Ron Hatton once took some pieces of Perspex from the cockpit housing of a crashed German plane in Buriton chalk pits – which were subsequently made into brooches for his mother!

Karin Antonini remembers two bombs dropped in the Hangers, while a friend of Dennis Geen was sitting on the beach at Hayling Island when a Messerschmitt flew by – the pilot waved to him and he waved back! Buster Hampton remembers stealing out of classrooms with his friends at Churcher's to sit underneath a low hedge near the Headmaster's office with a clear view over the Downs to watch the vapour trails as planes swept across the skies. Two Spitfires also crashed in Harrow Lane and Honeycritch Lane.

David Ellis has a remarkable photograph of a German plane which was shot down at Froxfield and which he had cycled up to see on the evening it crashed. John Pownall and his brother and mother also went to see it, but they were turned away at the entrance to the field by a policeman who whispered a warning to Mrs Pownall that it was not a sight for children – the pilot having been mutilated on crashing. Of course, such an event afforded little boys ample opportunities for salvaging pieces of the aircraft, just as others delighted in discovering pieces of shrapnel in their gardens after an aerial dogfight, or empty shell cases which frequently rained down from low-flying fighter planes as they shot at trains or cars. David Vincent's earliest memory of the war was accompanying his sister and mother to a field by the Jolly Sailor where, with a small wicker basket, they all collected empty bullet shell cases which had come down during a dogfight. These became toys for the children to play with.

A German bomber passed over Stroud one evening and dropped a bomb on the Roman villa, while a Lancaster bomber crashed at Liss Forest. Wilson Atkinson was stooking corn on his parents' farm in East Meon when he saw a German aircraft overhead open its bomb doors and drop a bomb, which was clearly aimed at nearby Leydene House, the home of HMS *Mercury*, the Navy's Signals centre:

A crashed Messerschmitt at Froxfield. (David Ellis Collection)

a few sheep were killed. Another bomber, a Bristol Blenheim, crashed in a field opposite the Seven Stars in Stroud.

Of course, the Heath Pond served as an ideal geographical reference point for enemy aircraft heading for Portsmouth or London. In fact, at the very beginning of the war, two or three Royal Engineers had come to test the depth of the water with a view to draining the Pond. However, this never happened. Most of the RAF sorties against the enemy bombers took place at night so many families found themselves spending their nights under the stairs! Another useful positioning strategy used by German planes was to light up the railway lines through Hampshire in order to find their way towards London. Nick Hall remembers seeing these flares at night from his bedroom window at the back of Fenns in Reservoir Lane, which backed on to the railway.

When German planes used the railway line as a directional guide for London and Portsmouth, trains would find themselves the targets of fighters. Other enemy planes might machine-gun main roads, and the main A3 would be a target for lone fighters with spare munitions or for low-flying Messerschmitts involved in dogfights with British planes. April Austin remembers the scary experience of hearing the tinkling of shell cases on the roof of their house in London Road, Sheet, as a plane with its machine-guns firing flew low overhead. She and her mother rushed into the cupboard under the stairs for protection, just as many families did at that time. An even more frightening experience came one day when she was waiting at the bus stop on London Road to go to school and, without warning, a plane came out of the clouds towards her; she had heard it firing its bullets on West Mark Camp seconds before and, as it approached her, it pulled up and away without firing again. This was clearly the same plane that had been seen by April's friends moments before as they approached Petersfield by train. The pilot had been machine-gunning down the railway line but, fortunately, had hit no-one. April returned home briefly to assure her mother that she was safe and then caught the next bus to school!

Mary Vincent was walking along Hylton Road with her father when a plane flew down low over the road – so she was hustled behind the nearest lamp post for protection! Margaret Childs, who worked for the Petersfield post office as a telephonist during the war years, remembers doing relief duty at the Liss office when Odette, the resistance heroine operating in France, was staying temporarily in Durford Wood and rang the telephone exchange to warn them that, if newspaper reporters rang, they were not to reveal her whereabouts.

David Martin's father had a lucky escape while driving from Petersfield to Liss: he was spotted by a German fighter pilot who decided to strafe the road at that moment; Mr Martin's life was saved by a bar of soap, wrapped in a parcel behind his driving seat, which took the impact of the one bullet that would otherwise have killed him.

Slowly, sadly, but inevitably, the war began to take its toll on human lives, especially those of servicemen who saw enemy action abroad. It was shortly after the retreat from Dunkirk in June 1940 that the first 'Killed in Action' notices began to appear in the *Squeaker*.

The Battle of the Atlantic is being lost!

The reasons why:

1. German U-boats, German bombers and the German fleet sink and seriously damage between them every month a total of 700 000 to 1 million tons of British and allied shipping.

2. All attempts at finding a satisfactory means of defence against the German U-boats or the German bombers have failed disastrously.

3. Even President Roosevelt has openly stated that for every five ships sunk by Germany, Britain and America between them can only build two new ones. All attempts to launch a larger shipbuilding programme in America have failed.

4. Britain is no longer in a position to secure her avenues of supply. The population of Britain has to do with about half the ration that the population of Germany gets. Britain, herself, can only support 40 % of her population from her own resources in spite of the attempts made to increase the amount of land under cultivation. If the war is continued until 1942, 60 % of the population of Britain will starve!

All this means that starvation in Britain is not to be staved off. At the most it can be postponed, but whether starvation comes this year or at the beginning of next doesn't make a ha'porth of difference. Britain must starve because she is being cut off from her supplies.

Britain's losing the Battle of the Atlantic means

Britain's losing the war!

German propaganda collected by David Ellis after the Workhouse bombing. (David Ellis Collection)

In July 1940 the Urban District Council considered the construction of public air-raid shelters on Petersfield Heath, but no decision was taken on the issue. There was a suggestion that the old brewery in College Street be adapted for such use, but local rates would have to rise to pay for the shelters as Petersfield was not, in government parlance, 'situated in one of the certain specified areas' to qualify for subsidy. The question of air-raid shelters was brought up again at the Council's September meeting and, after a plea from the Headmistress of the Junior Council School who said that parents of pupils would be happier to send their children to school if there were shelters for them on the premises, the County Emergency Committee approved a proposal to use the basement of the old brewery, which could house just over two hundred people. The Council did stress, however, that as far as possible people should use their cellars rather than depend on the Council to build completely new shelters in the town.

August 1940 saw the biggest air raid to date on the city and the dockyards of Portsmouth. In Petersfield the Chairman of the ARP Committee appealed for more wardens, required because of the increased number of raids and therefore an increase in the number of hours of duty. Keith Gammon, Chairman of the UDC, reported that they had decided to establish a 'Spitfire Fund' in Petersfield, the slogan reading:

> 12 pennies make a shilling
> 20 shillings make a pound
> 5000 pounds make one Spitfire
> 1 Spitfire spells one Messerschmitt.

Under the terms of the National Service Act of 1939 every male between the ages of eighteen and forty-one became liable for military service. This was extended in 1941 for both men and women to the age of fifty-one, although in practice no men over the age of forty-five were conscripted. Men in reserved occupations such as farmers, teachers, factory workers or those in specialist trades relating to the war effort were exempt. Those who, out of principle, became conscientious objectors, found themselves working particularly hard but, although it has been calculated that they represented only about 0.7 per cent of all men registered, they did not suffer the same persecution which had confronted the group of 'conchies' in the First World War. Edward Barnsley, the Froxfield furniture maker, had become a pacifist after the First World War and, with his wife Tania, who admired Gandhi and was a fervent follower of the Peace Pledge Union, started a group for local conscientious objectors, of which there were perhaps ten or twelve at any one time. One occupation which absorbed this group of people was forestry, another was teaching, another farming. The Barnsley workshop closed down during the war and became a first-aid point, as most of the staff went into the Services or worked in munitions factories in Portsmouth. Edward and Tania Barnsley also organised the regular delivery to London's East End of surplus fruit and vegetables from the Steep and Petersfield area.

THE WORKHOUSE BOMBING

In November 1940 there came an incident which no one present in the town at the time will ever forget. It was if not the only then certainly the most devastating event which Petersfield was to witness during the whole of the war. It was also the only occasion when an enemy bomb was launched specifically at the town.

Late on the morning of 21 November the Petersfield Public Institution in the town, generally known by its Victorian name of the workhouse, and situated officially at 1 Ramshill, was bombed. There had been no time for an air-raid warning to be sounded. Several accounts of this incident have been recorded, but from the many eye-witnesses it is clear that a single plane, a Heinkel 111, had dropped a bomb from a low height, scoring a direct hit on the workhouse.

The damage to the workhouse was extensive: the entire front of the building was demolished, as was part of the centre including the main entrance hall, the one-storey porter's quarters on the side, some stores, a portion of the master's apartments behind and some old casual wards close to the main building. Sadly for historians, a great number of Petersfield's records dating from the stagecoach era were lost in the bombing – the sorting of these documents had been left to the Petersfield Scouts, as they had become responsible for all the paper salvage operations in the town at that time.

More tragically, the bomb killed seven inmates, all but one of them elderly, including the Master, Mr Wilfrid Ixer, who had served there for twenty-eight years and the Porter, Mr Arthur Weeks, who had twenty-one years of service to the Institution. Regrettably, Mr Ixer's wife, who was also the Institution's Matron, succumbed to her injuries and died a few days later. It was perhaps fortunate that the bomb mainly destroyed the office side of the building, otherwise there would have been far more casualties.

Although highly unlikely, it is just feasible that, as many accounts testify, the reason for dropping the bomb was the nearby presence of Emanuel School JTC (Junior Training Corps) – from 1940 the new name for the old OTC (Officers' Training Corps) – whose cadets were drilling in Churcher's playground. However, it is far more likely that the bomber was aiming at the nearby railway station in order to disrupt supply lines to and from London.

Accounts of the many and varied effects of the bomb are vivid. Joan Norris, a maid to the Britnell family whose house, Oakfield, was rendered uninhabitable by the blast, probably owed her life to Rex, a black Labrador whose barking alerted two young men coming along Love Lane to help, then indicating the spot where she was lying buried and unconscious below the debris. Rex was subsequently awarded a collar by the RSPCA for his act of heroism.

At Downleaze (Girls) School close by the railway arch across the bottom of Ramshill, about a hundred yards from where the bomb dropped, glass imploded into the classrooms. At Winton House, then a small Dame school, the blast blew a blackboard off its easel. At Churcher's, David Ellis was in classroom E, which overlooked the workhouse, and saw the plane drop the bomb and some

The former Workhouse, now an award-winning housing complex. (Author's Collection)

accompanying propaganda leaflets, a few of which he managed to retrieve. These warned Britons of the imminent threat of starvation because of the alleged success of U-boats in blocking their food supplies.

The Churcher's senior boys, who were asked to go and help after the bombing, found belongings scattered across their playing fields; at a cottage opposite the workhouse April Austin saw a bath hanging half off one floor with the burst pipes gushing water everywhere while in the garden a telephone was hanging from a tree. June Brooks, who also lived at Ramshill, was blown out of the armchair where she had been reading a book. The impact of the explosion threw Mrs Fitt from her chair and a clock from the wall in her house in College Street.

On hearing the explosion Mrs Bennetts, the Headmistress of Sheet School, called the children in from the playground. Afterwards she saw debris scattered from Love Lane as far as the school. Meanwhile, at the County High School, little flakes of ceilingite fluttered down on the pupils when the bomb exploded. Branches were stripped from a tree some 10 feet beyond the main entrance door of the workhouse, apple trees were uprooted from a garden opposite and windows of houses hundreds of yards away were shattered. Curiously sickening was the sight of every branch of the aforementioned tree festooned with clothing and other materials blown on to it from a storeroom behind the hall of the Institution.

The *Squeaker*, oddly, carried two reports on this incident. The first appeared a week after the event, detailing the effects of the bombing and the names of the inmates who had been killed; the second, a week later, as if to conform retrospectively to a news blackout order, merely mentioned the damage done to an 'institution in a Southern town'. It did, however, mention the great help afforded by the boys of 'a local secondary school' who had worked on 'untiringly, even after the others had stopped'. What was more significant, perhaps, was the comment from a correspondent who expressed the hope that 'out of this evil act, good may come'. He described the workhouse as an eyesore, suggesting that the old folk in it, who had spent their lives in hard labouring jobs, 'deserved a better fate than being herded in such barrack-like structures, relics of the bad old days of Bumbledom'. Presumably also in the interests of security, the first of these reports obliquely referred to the workhouse as 'a Public Assistance Institution' in 'a market town'.

The need for an instant response to this incident, which had made several inmates of the Institution homeless, led to the Methodist Hall being transformed into a ward with beds for the geriatric patients from the workhouse. In addition Mr A.J. Wilkins, the Urban District Council's Billeting Officer, immediately commandeered St Peter's hall as emergency sleeping accommodation. The members of the public who arrived at the hall later that evening for a whist drive found the place filled with beds and old men sitting up in them!

For those who were present in Petersfield that November the bombing of the workhouse made a great impact, not least for its horrific consequences in the immediate neighbourhood of Ramshill. As the premises were rendered uninhabitable they were used later to house supplies of emergency food and other stores, as was the cellar of the Old College nearby. Part of the remaining buildings was also used as a nursery school.

Shortly after this event another less hazardous bombing took place in the town. The *Squeaker*, limited by wartime censorship in not being able to name Petersfield specifically and anxious to deny the enemy any success with this mission, reported the bombing under the heading 'Harmless bomb dropping' as follows:

A few nights ago, a string of explosive bombs was dropped in some open meadows to the south of a market town in one of the Southern Counties, but, fortunately, did no damage. They fell not far from a hospital, vicarage, and other residences.

This tends to support the view that there were several bombs dropped that same night, and Vicky Ball remembers the crater in the field known as Moggs Mead, slightly to the south of the workhouse, which could well have been caused by the plane jettisoning its unused bombs before returning across the Channel to Germany. This was not an uncommon feature of enemy bombing in both urban and rural areas during the war.

The Old College, College Street, as it looked during the war. (Author's Collection)

CHRISTMAS 1940

Entertainments in the town for Christmas 1940 continued to display the optimistic note which had persisted for a year already. In its characteristically formal way the *Squeaker* reported as follows:

> Of the spirit and manner in which Christmas was observed in Petersfield and the district there is not very much to record, except to note that it was spent very quietly, and what was the chief cause for thankfulness, entirely without any evil visitation or disturbance from the sky.

Mindful of the moral obligation to its visitors at this (theoretically) festive time, Petersfield extended its hospitality to its temporary visitors, members of the Forces and evacuees. There was little in the way of public entertainment except for the Savoy cinema which was, naturally, well patronised. 'Saturday morning pictures' continued to be the highlight of the week for many children and Mr Percy Lambert's 'Little Wonder' red bus brought patrons in from Buriton for this. The 'Little Wonder' bus was garaged in The Spain and could be hired by families for short journeys in the area – to go to Hayling Island, for example.

At the Drill Hall in Dragon Street (on the site now occupied by The Maltings), the Christmas celebrations were traditional 'even to the stirring of Christmas puddings'. The crowds of soldiers decorated the hall themselves with two Christmas trees and fairy lights; on 22 December carols were sung by a large audience of servicemen and were accompanied by the Petersfield String Orchestra, conducted by Mrs Kathleen Money-Chappelle. The canteen was open on Christmas Day too, when several hundred people enjoyed the organised games and dancing, and free food was supplied throughout the evening. But the celebrations reached their peak on Boxing Day, when practically two hundred men sat down to a Christmas dinner of turkey and plum pudding, with crackers, sweets, cigarettes, fruit and nuts also being provided. Mrs Money-Chappelle and her band of helpers were toasted and a carnival dance followed the dinner until midnight, with the Drill Hall Band in attendance. The cost of these entertainments was met by the Christmas Cheer Fund, collected from individuals and from the Drill Hall events prior to Christmas.

On New Year's Eve a New Year carnival ball was held to close the festive season at the Drill Hall. Meanwhile, in the Town Hall and in St Peter's church there were concerts; a New Year social and dance was held at the Women's Cooperative Guild; another dance in aid of 'Comforts for the Troops' took place in the Drill Hall; and a YWCA Dance at St Peter's hall invited the attendance of civilians for just 1*s*, and troops for 6*d*.

Nor had the Christmas spirit deserted the schools: the Misses Richardson's pupils at Ling Riggs School (at 5 Sandringham Road), for example, put on an entertainment for parents and friends.

Many London families chose to have their children remain in Petersfield at this time because of the Blitz raging in the capital. So it was that, in many cases, Emanuel boys and Battersea girls experienced real family life and their acceptance as family members during the festive season.

CHAPTER THREE
1941

Daily Life

THE DEVELOPING WAR SITUATION

The worst raid of the war so far on the Portsmouth area occurred on 10 January 1941. The high explosive and incendiary bombs which fell on Portsmouth, Southsea, Portsmouth Harbour, Fratton and Gosport had the effect of bringing all traffic to a halt. As the situation became ever more precarious and untenable for many hundreds of Portsmouth residents, now refugees in their own city, Clanfield was turned into a kind of shanty town, where people escaping the bombing and devastation began to set up temporary homes in railway carriages, buses or wooden shacks. Some sought asylum elsewhere and those families of better means managed to come as far as Petersfield to settle either temporarily or permanently. Mr A.J. Wilkins, the Billeting Officer in Petersfield, 'borrowed' the Midhurst train (the 'Middy') as temporary accommodation for the refugees. As it was always parked in sidings overnight at Petersfield station, it was fair game for him! With a good supply of blankets from his store, his *ad hoc* arrangements served the homeless well until he could find them more permanent addresses. Young children arriving in the wake of the Portsmouth blitz were housed temporarily in the Infants' School in St Peter's Road (where St Peter's Court now stands).

The Middy, the train which ran between Petersfield, Midhurst and Pulborough alongside the River Rother, was a one-carriage affair, powered by a steam locomotive that pushed the carriage to Midhurst and pulled it back again. It ran from Petersfield 'Junction' over the railway bridge across the old A3 at the bottom of Ramshill, where sections of the old embankment can still be seen by Madeline Road, the Community Centre and at the rear of houses on the Herne Farm estate and Durford Road. It provided a valuable service during the war years and was much missed when the line was axed in 1955, almost exactly a century after Petersfield station was opened. As for the railway bridge over Ramshill, it was superfluous by the mid-1950s and was blown up – an operation which required a great deal of effort before the bridge finally succumbed.

The two Council schools (Senior and Junior) in St Peter's Road were equipped for the reception and comfort of refugee families by voluntary organisations such as the Red Cross, the WVS (Women's Voluntary Service) canteen and the ARP, while the Food Office staff organised the distribution of ration books and food for them. An urgent appeal was made for clothing for these people, especially the children, who had lost all or nearly everything in the bombing of Portsmouth during December 1940 and January 1941.

At the end of 1940 there were nearly seven hundred householders in the Petersfield Rural District who were hosting evacuees, and a report by Sir Hugh

Cocke on the government evacuation scheme as it affected the Petersfield area concluded that 'the way evacuation was being carried out was quite wonderful'. Early in January 1941, immediately after the Portsmouth blitz, a large number of people from the city would come up to Petersfield hoping to find accommodation each night; Rowland, Son and Vincent, for example, had some premises (behind the actual shop) where they could house about forty to fifty people in the roof space.

As to the war effort, Churcher's College stated that they were 'still largely military-minded', with about a hundred pupils participating in army-style camps with the Cadet Corps and some others having joined the very active local unit of the Air Training Corps. Some boys combined pleasure with profit by learning to drive Fordson tractors or work in the Youth Service Squads as foresters and hop-pickers, or simply helping local farmers with potato planting and lifting, or harvest work in the summer holidays.

In Petersfield a new fire station was built in 1941 at the corner of Heath Road near the Town Hall (now part of Herne Court), which was able to house the three fire vehicles belonging to the (former) AFS as well as two ambulances, thus centralising the emergency services in one spot in the town. In fact, it was in 1941 that the National Fire Service was created out of the numerous fire authorities in the country and, at the same time, steps were taken by the government to provide an Emergency Water Supply in the form of static water tanks in towns and villages. These were to provide supplies of water for fire-fighters in case of incendiary

The Middy, 1953. (Author's Collection)

attack, and for householders who were without a good supply in the home. Three such tanks were erected in Petersfield: outside St Peter's church, at the bottom of Bell Hill and by the railway station.

On the military front 1941 was a hard year: there were defeats in Malaya, Singapore and Burma, and setbacks in North Africa. As a result food rationing became stricter at home. Churchill had become Prime Minister in May 1940 and the change of atmosphere produced in the country by the new Coalition government was almost tangible. In the Petersfield telephone exchange, as elsewhere in the country, there was a noticeable absence of telephone activity during Churchill's speeches, followed by a surge immediately afterwards.

Don and Phil Eades and John Lovell remember some bombs falling close to The Causeway at the bottom of Bolinge Hill, one of which shattered the roof of the Mackie family house, and another landing in a line of conifers, creating a gap in the trees which can still be seen today. Apart from some other properties in The Causeway losing some roof slates, no serious damage was caused and there was no loss of life. The local farm manager went to look at the damage the next morning and found his cows staring into a large crater – but none of the cows had been hit! Most of these incidents occurred at night, when the German bombers were attacking Portsmouth under the relative cover of darkness.

Another indirect consequence of the war affecting life in Petersfield was the brief stop made on one occasion at the Red Lion Inn by a coach carrying badly burned RAF aircrew en route from London to a specialist burns unit at Haslar Hospital. Over six hundred pilots were wounded by fire during the Battle of Britain. June Brooks relates how her mother had been asked to organise lunch for these men, who called themselves 'The Guinea Pig Club', probably because of the innovative treatment for burns they were about to undergo. In view of the fact that Petersfield youngsters of the time were more used to enjoying themselves in the Chinese Room upstairs, the makeshift trestle tables set out in the dining room (now the long bar) downstairs for the airmen shows the extent to which the war impinged on Petersfield's relative normality in wartime.

THE 'HOME FROM HOME' UNITED SERVICES CANTEEN & SOCIAL CLUB

In January 1941 the Urban District Council discussed the urgent need for a communal 'feeding centre' in Petersfield for the (mainly Portsmouth) refugees and those families with evacuated children who found it difficult to provide regular meals for them. Since the Territorial Army Drill Hall was shortly to be handed over to the Home Guard as a training centre, one provision for public meals in Petersfield would be lost. Kathleen Money-Chappelle, who had previously run a simple café in St Peter's Hall for soldiers, and then, with a £5 donation for buying tables and chairs, had moved to the Drill Hall when the troops became too numerous, now found herself without a 'home' for her customers. The Drill Hall had been in use for about eighteen months, in which time it had grown to be an all-day canteen, serving some two thousand men weekly. After the first big blitz on Portsmouth, however, it had also become a food station for several hundred refugees.

In a letter to the editor of the *Squeaker* in February 1941 Sapper McGuire called the closure of the Drill Hall canteen in Dragon Street a tragedy, and wrote of its 'unique atmosphere, which combined homeliness, understanding, efficiency and straight dealing with that of comradeship'. The old canteen had been a centre of service, social life and recreation for soldiers, sailors, Marines, Air Force, Dominions and Colonial troops from a wide area; it was also a recognised stopping place for military transport on the main London to Portsmouth road.

It was at this moment that Mrs Money-Chappelle began to negotiate for a site in the centre of town on which a temporary building for the purpose could be erected to carry on the work of the Drill Hall canteen. She sought to replace the old canteen with her 'Home from Home', a non-profit-making venture owned by Trustees, which at the end of the war would be placed on the market and the money realised

Laying the foundation stones of the Home from Home canteen. (Petersfield Museum)

The opening ceremony of the Home from Home canteen in College Street with the band of the Royal Marines. (Petersfield Museum)

given to a Services Charity. The principles of the canteen were that all profits made should go back into the canteen in the form of recreational facilities for the troops.

She wrote to the *Squeaker* appealing for funds for such a canteen and was delighted when a response came from Messrs Filer, who owned the land previously occupied by the old brewery in College Street (burned down in 1934), donating the site for the duration of the war. Again thanks to the *Squeaker*, which reported regularly on the development plans for the 'Home from Home' and which advertised its various fund-raising activities, money began to come in from public and private sources for its Building Fund. Lists of donors were published at regular intervals in the paper and there were numerous dances, variety entertainments, musical afternoons and concert parties organised to raise money for, and awareness of, the new venture.

Interior of the Home from Home canteen. (Money-Chappelle Collection)

It was a testament to Mrs Money-Chappelle's perseverance and determination that there was sufficient money available for the foundation stone to be laid four months later, in June, and for the opening ceremony to be performed that August. Funds continued to pour in and Flora Twort, the Petersfield artist, offered to execute sketches for 1 guinea during a week in September 1941, the proceeds from which were to go to the Home from Home Canteen Fund. So Mrs Money-Chappelle's initiative rapidly bore fruit and the inauguration of the new canteen was a grand affair: the Lord Lieutenant of the County, Lord Mottistone, performed the opening ceremony, alongside the MP for East Hants, General Sir George Jeffreys. Also present were six detachments of HM Forces representing the Navy, Canadian and New Zealand armies, the Royal Engineers, the RAOC, the RAF, and the ATS (Auxiliary Territorial Service), as well as leading residents in Petersfield who had subscribed to the scheme. There was a march past and civic reception at the Town Hall and a parade through the town led by the Band of the Royal Marines from Portsmouth. Mrs Money-Chappelle's cousin, Canon W.T. Money, a founder member of 'Toc H' after the First World War whose

Exterior of the Home from Home canteen. (Money-Chappelle Collection)

parish was now in Greenwich, had agreed to become the Honorary Chaplain of the Home from Home canteen, and Lord Horder, of Ashford Chace, Physician to King George V and VI, became Chairman of the Advisory Committee.

Soldiers based at Longmoor Camp (Royal Engineers), Bordon (Canadians), Air Force personnel from Telegraph Hill, sailors recuperating at Leydene House in East Meon, Free French Navy personnel on leave at Steep House, together with Czechs, Poles and REMEs, all met at the canteen. Later there were also Americans from Tichborne, Ropley and other country areas. The canteen itself provided the necessary buses to transport the men from the various camps in the area in and out of Petersfield, where they would head for the pubs, cinema or the Home from Home canteen. (According to one estimate there were forty-one pubs in Petersfield in those days!)

Thus the atmosphere in the canteen was highly cosmopolitan, with many languages being spoken. The French Navy troops, part of the Free French Forces under General de Gaulle in London, came up regularly from the fleet in Portsmouth to Steep House, where Madame Maze ran a rest and recuperation centre for them.

Steep House during the war when it served as a rest centre for the Free French Navy. (Author's Collection)

Madame Maze was the sister-in-law of Colonel Paul Maze, who had given his open tourer to the Home Guard. Some enterprising girls from Petersfield High School cunningly supplemented their French classes by coming to chat to the Frenchmen on occasions. Maisie Hobbs remembers seeing the sailors in their smart red, white and blue uniforms coming down Tilmore Road into town. There were also some sailors from the Free Dutch Navy housed in Steep; both the French and the Dutch tended to stay in the rest centres in Steep rather than risk going to their homes in occupied countries. Mary Stace remembers finding it most interesting talking to the troops from many different countries who, although not officers (who tended to go to other pubs and restaurants like the Red Lion), did represent a fair cross-section of the middle and working classes from Britain and abroad.

Evidently Kathleen Money-Chappelle had been the epitome of the concept of the right person in the right place at the right time.

KATHLEEN MONEY-CHAPPELLE

Kathleen Money-Chappelle was born in 1898, the daughter of Charles Money, a globetrotting, ex-Indian Army old Etonian whose family home was at Northbrook Cottage, College Street, Petersfield, and his wife Kathleen Grantham, twenty-six years his junior. The young Kathleen soon earned a reputation as a singer: in the First World War she visited Portsmouth hospitals where, being too young at first to become a nurse, she entertained the patients with their favourite contemporary songs. A little later she did in fact join the Queen Alexandra Royal Nursing Corps and served briefly in France. After the war she worked in a quartermaster's store in Portsmouth, distributing clothes to soldiers as they returned from the Front, a miserable sight, and one which clearly influenced her sympathetic treatment of troops later in her life. As her son David has said, 'she understood soldiery very well'.

In the interwar years, despite having no previous teaching experience, but clearly with a natural talent for piano playing and singing, she was appointed music teacher at the recently opened Petersfield County High School for Girls, where she remained from 1920 to 1925, thereafter pursuing her studies at the Royal Academy of Music in London. She later formed the Petersfield Glee Club for amateur singers. However, it was a great source of frustration and dismay to her that she herself was not able to sing for seven years; she had caught a virus while working at the Portsmouth clothing store and was obliged to undergo an operation on her throat. This had affected her vocal cords and so she was sadly robbed of her greatest natural talent. In addition to this cruel misfortune, she suffered badly from her height: at over 6 feet tall, she was prone to some curvature of the spine, and this made it difficult for her to play the piano without pain. Nevertheless, her own physical problems did not prevent her from exercising another of her talents: that of organising others and, in particular, of creating choirs whenever and wherever the opportunity arose.

She married Arthur Chappelle, an Army Officer, in 1925 and they settled in North End, Portsmouth, where she taught piano, drama and elocution. They changed their name by Deed Poll to Money-Chappelle shortly afterwards. Later, Kathleen opened studios in London, Southsea and Petersfield, where her choirs often sang in festivals and competitions. In 1931 she joined her husband in Hong Kong where she studied Chinese music, formed the Hong Kong Ladies' Choir, and lectured on Chinese radio. Meanwhile, her husband had been posted to Palestine, but Mrs Money-Chappelle returned to Petersfield in 1938, bringing with her daughter Mary, now aged three, and her five-year-old son David. During the six years of the war she organised first the Drill Hall canteen, then the Home from Home United Services Canteen and Social Club in College Street.

After the war she continued to organise celebrity concerts and conducted and directed plays, operas and musicals. Her life's ambition – her own school – was achieved in 1947 when she began the Petersfield School of Music and Drama at 24 High Street and subsequently, from 1972, at her new home at 72 Station Road (The Laurels). When she died in 1979, only a few hundred yards from where she had been born, there were still over a hundred pupils on her books.

Kathleen Money-Chappelle. (Money-Chappelle Collection)

DEVELOPMENTS IN PUBLIC SERVICES

Another development in the welfare of Petersfield inhabitants came about later in 1941. At a public meeting held in March there was a call for the establishment of a Citizens' Advice Bureau in the town. There were at the time around a thousand CABs in the country as a whole. In Petersfield, some fast decisions were made and by April a new bureau had already opened its doors, giving advice to the townspeople on personal and domestic matters. In the first two months of its existence, it dealt with 276 enquiries. These mainly concerned individual evacuation and billeting problems but unfortunately, given the local conditions for these, it was stated that very little could be done to help these people in the wartime circumstances. Despite its limitations, however, the CAB did some valuable work in the community: it helped with individual case papers, answered general enquiries and transmitted Red Cross messages to and from servicemen and women; in the first five years of its existence, the CAB dealt with around two thousand problems each year.

Mr A.J. Wilkins, the Billeting Officer for the Urban District Council, naturally had a very busy war. He had special powers which enabled him to issue his own petrol coupons for his staff who needed to use their cars to find accommodation for evacuees; he also had the power of requisition and took over premises to use as hostels for children; he found the staff to care for them; and his office also ran a small hospital. He talks of seeing 'the seamy side of life', dealing with the billeting and welfare of hundreds of children, expectant mothers and folks blitzed out of bombed areas. His equanimity must have been stretched a little when he found himself unwittingly running a brothel in The Spain, the occupants of which were ladies of easy virtue from London's East End, who had a constant source of customers from the Canadian troops stationed at Bramshott!

A further request for public amenities in Petersfield came from the Divisional Food Office in Reading, which suggested that a British Restaurant be set up in the town, and in September the Urban District Council heard that the Ministry of Food had approved this measure. A hut for the purpose was to be built behind the Town Hall.

In London the Ministry of Supply exercised its power to requisition all unnecessary iron and steel for scrap; in Petersfield notice was served of a survey of all such items as railings, chains, bollards, gates and stiles to help in the war effort, although railings of special artistic merit or historic value were excluded. David Ellis remembers the railings in front of his house in Sheet being removed for scrap and he himself took part in the collection of saucepans for their aluminium content.

Petersfield now had a new Member of Parliament, General Sir George Jeffreys, who took over the seat vacated by Sir Reginald Dorman-Smith. General Jeffreys had been the Commanding Officer to Winston Churchill (then a Major) in the First World War. He entered Westminster in March.

The latest population returns for the Petersfield Urban District area at this time showed an increase from approximately 12,000 in January 1940 to nearly 20,000 in January 1941, both figures due principally, of course, to the large number of

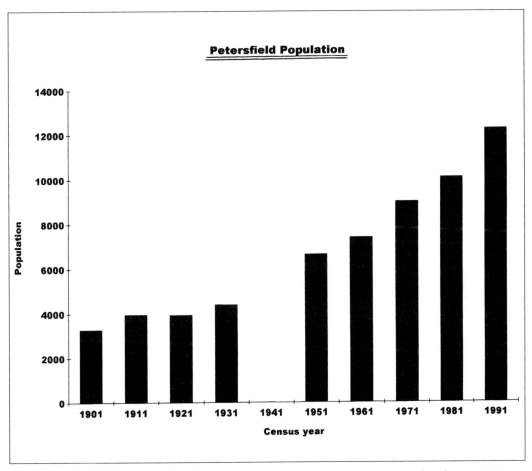

Petersfield Population

Census figures showing the growing population of Petersfield. No census was undertaken in 1941 because of the war. (Author's Collection)

evacuees in the town, who caused the official figures to double in the war years. At the end of the war the population was to decrease again almost to its pre-war level. Although no national census was undertaken in 1941, the statistics from 1931 and 1951 indicate that the population of the town had risen from 4,387 to 6,626 in this twenty-year period, roughly proportional to the general, steadily rising trend in the fifty-year period between 1921 and 1971.

The death was announced in July 1941 of Captain Percy William Seward, JP. The Seward family had been prominent in Petersfield since their arrival in Weston in 1805. Captain Seward's father, Colonel Samuel Seward, had been the last mayor of the old Borough of Petersfield. After an active military career with the 3rd Volunteers (Hants) regiment and later during the South African war of 1900 Captain Seward, a farmer and sheep breeder by profession, went into public service in Petersfield, becoming a County Councillor, the Chairman of the Rural District Council, a JP and Chairman of the Governors of Churcher's College.

Misdemeanours & Miscreants

Naturally the war did not prevent the inevitable rivalries between children, especially boys, and Norma Collins and Graeme Triggs both recount the more or less innocuous confrontations between Sheet schoolchildren and Churcher's College boys: Graeme remembers the bus journey to Steep; as the bus passed Churcher's at the top of Ramshill, the song would ring out:

> Churcher's College got no knowledge,
> `Only made of bread and porridge!

while at Inman's Road in Sheet the village schoolboys used to throw stones at the Churcher's boys as they came home from school.

Despite the apparently overwhelming success of the billeting of evacuee schoolchildren in the town, some misdemeanours obviously occurred. The local branch of the RSPCA had written to the UDC to complain of evacuee children interfering with animals on market days in The Square. The Honorary Secretary said that 'town children knew nothing about the right treatment of animals and they (the animals) got excited and difficult to control'. However, when a stray pig made its way into the High Street there were seventy or eighty children of all ages chasing after it, screaming, shouting and laughing, and for some time they impeded any practical efforts to catch the distracted animal. The children were said to have behaved like 'thoughtless young barbarians'.

Under the heading 'Youngsters in trouble' the *Squeaker* published a report concerning a number of offences perpetrated by some youths (not all Petersfielders, nor all evacuees) who had been charged with a variety of misdeeds, including stealing a bike, carrying an unlicensed airgun, displaying a bedroom light and even 'damaging growing onions'!

Youngsters were not the only miscreants of the time: in November 1941 a farmer was summoned before local magistrates for allowing 'cows without lights fore and aft' to be conducted along the Petersfield Road!

On the question of children (or, indeed, troops) bathing in the Heath Pond, which was raised at a meeting of the Petersfield Urban District Council in July 1941, Mr Percy Burley, the Clerk, explained that there were no regulations beyond the fact that bathers must be suitably attired. Steve Pibworth used to help Sam de Cart with his boat hire business on the Heath Pond and remembers the (often drunken) soldiers in boats which they capsized, thus falling into the water and losing their gas masks – a heinous offence!

It was perhaps inevitable that the proximity of young soldiers from local camps mixing with evacuee schoolgirls from London would lead to some problems in Petersfield where they both congregated for their entertainments. The small number of girls who became pregnant, a social disgrace at this time, were returned to their homes and left the town for good.

Livestock for sale in the market, outside the post office. (Wilson Atkinson Collection)

LIVESTOCK

Throughout the 1930s Petersfield saw approximately 15,000 cattle and other animals for sale annually at its market. During the Second World War 1941 represented a peak year, thanks mainly to the very high number of sheep and lambs sold. (The last cattle market in Petersfield was held in 1962.)

DATE	CATTLE	CALVES	SHEEP & LAMBS	PIGS	TOTALS
1940	2,204	2,087	1,897	3,271	9,459
1941	1,897	3,555	7,360	1,299	14,111
1942	1,725	3,170	5,494	1,878	12,267
1943	1,636	3,458	3,146	1,881	10,121
1944	1,601	3,417	2,903	1,467	9,388
1945	1,804	3,548	2,857	1,779	9,988

Petersfield as an old market town held a great attraction for local inhabitants, despite the restrictions of the war. Many people who remember those years talk affectionately of the old lifestyle of the farmers and cattle traders, the drovers, the auctioneers (the chief auctioneer being Alan Hinxman of Hall, Pain and Foster), and of the animals themselves. George Money, one member of the large Money family in Petersfield at that time, and Charles Anstey, connected to the Gander (the High Street butchers) family, served as Mr Hinxman's assistants, rounding up the cattle, leading them in front of the auctioneer and generally supervising the animals during the sales. Children used to go to the poultry market 'just for fun' to see the animals and listen to the auctioneer (Mr Hunt of Jacobs and Hunt).

Cattle sometimes escaped the clutches of the drovers at the market; they needed to pass through Lavant Street on their way to and from the station, and on one occasion a bull got away and charged into Mr Freeman's hairdressing shop at 17 Chapel Street, making its way behind the counter and causing general mayhem before being rescued by the drover! It was not everybody who appreciated the presence of such large animals in the centre of town, however, despite their initial attraction to onlookers and casual visitors. Maisie Hobbs once complained to a drover about the tight restriction of movement for the cows, which were tied to the railings outside the church, but the drover swore at her and an argument ensued. Norma Collins was another who took the farmers to task if she felt the animals were being badly treated.

Likewise, cattle arriving at Petersfield station on their way to the abattoir had to be driven down the top end of Lavant Street, then right into Charles Street – another hazardous undertaking – and this again sometimes led to some hair-raising escapades. The occasional bull who declined to make the right turn continued down Lavant Street and occasionally 'shopped' – once in Martin and Triggs, the outfitters, and another time in Mr Emm's shop with crates of china on display outside . . . the proverbial became the reality in Lavant Street, Petersfield!

RATIONING

Through an article in the *Squeaker* the Urban District Council Food Officer reminded everyone of the regulations regarding food rationing and warned that, owing to the slightly unequal distribution of food nationally, more rationing would be introduced. It was clear that those with time on their hands could 'shop crawl' and buy up extra supplies of unrationed food displayed in the shops. This was seen to be an injustice and, consequently, such produce as cheese and preserves would henceforth be rationed. Equally, some shopkeepers were refusing to sell goods to unregistered customers and, although they were entitled to do this, it would benefit everybody if the public only used those shops where they were officially registered. As the end of the second year of the war was approaching the Ministry of Food reminded people of the general position regarding food supply:

Opposite: *Flora Twort's watercolour of the poultry market, which was behind the post office.* *(Hampshire Museums Service)*

The things that they cannot get, the tomatoes that they just missed, the strawberries that have disappeared into the jam factories, the potatoes that have failed in the gap between the two crops, are in the front of the picture and naturally cause much irritation. But how often do people remember the things that we have been able to get with unfailing regularity through these two years of war; haven't we all been able to get our regular weekly ration, our meat, bacon, butter, sugar, fats, and tea? Does everyone realise that we are the only country at war which has been able to increase its rations, is trebling the cheese ration, has doubled the jam ration from August, increased the meat ration lately, taken offal off the ration and given extra sugar for jam-making in the month of July?

As if to encourage people to believe in the efficiency of the Ministry, and in order to allay fears about future food supplies, it stressed that it was stocking necessities for the next winter: refrigeration space was said to be full of stocks of meat and other foods, canned beef was in good supply, there were large reserves of wheat in the country and supplies of canned and dried milk were also in store. Thanks for all these supplies were due to the Royal Navy and the Merchant Navy who operated vital convoys across the Atlantic.

Food rationing was controlled strictly by a ration-book system. Approximate amounts available (these varied during the course of the war) were (per person, per week):

Bacon or ham: 4–8 oz	Tea : 2–4 oz
Cheese: 1–8 oz	Sugar: 8–16 oz
Butter: 1–8 oz	Sweets and chocolate: 2–4 oz
Eggs: ½–4	Milk: ½–2 pints
National Dried Milk: 1 tin (4 pints) every 4 weeks	
Dried eggs: 1 packet (12 eggs) every 8 weeks	

For those in charge of meals for schoolchildren, there were administrative difficulties to overcome. Susie Fisher, in charge of the kitchen at Adhurst St Mary as well as teaching some Domestic Science at the school, had 140 ration books to take each week to the UDC Food Office located at 66 Station Road. There were fewer problems than one might imagine here: meat, for example, which might have been a shortage commodity, was plentiful, owing partly to the presence of some vegetarians among the pupils, and partly to the availability of a limited amount of meat on the farm at Adhurst itself. Susie Fisher would put a weekly menu up on display because civil servants from London used to come down occasionally to check on the children's diet.

Dorothy Coombes worked at the Food Office from 1943 to 1949. Backroom work involved assessing the amounts of rationed goods going to all the food suppliers in the area, according to the number of adults and children registered, and taking into account the extra rations for agricultural workers and people with

Children fed on wartime rations seen at the Town Hall, with Keith Gammon, chairman of the UDC, in the centre of the front row. (Author's Collection)

certain types of illness. The area was enormous: it stretched from Lovedean in the south to Grayshott in the north. Each retailer had to supply the Food Office with the names and addresses of wholesalers for each commodity and permits were written out each month. Catering establishments in the same area, with its population of around 26,000, had to supply monthly numbers of meals served. This work was so crucial to the fair distribution of food that the Food Office's store of ration books was kept safely in a cell at Petersfield Police Station, and in order for the staff to check stocks and collect the books a taxi was arranged to escort them to and from the police station!

Upstairs in the same Food Office was the office dealing with the issue of National Identity Cards. First Mrs Lunt, then Mrs Hobbs, looked after categorising everyone according to their age, nationality, type of job, their length of stay in Petersfield and other details. At the end of the war food rationing continued for a further seven years and then another Ministry took over the Food Office, this time dealing with the Valuation of Property.

Clothes rationing also drove people to extraordinary inventiveness: Mary Stace's dressmaker made her a coat out of a blanket; Shirley George made skirts out of blackout material, because this was not limited by the rationing strictures; the best ladies' underwear originated from parachute silk. Nick Hall's mother made him an elf's outfit from (brown) blackout material for him to wear on stage when his junior school put on an entertainment for parents. (Was this prescience on the part of his mother in guiding her son towards his future business of theatrical costume hire?) The clamour for blackout curtains and blinds – for the schools as well as for individuals – meant a twelve-hour working day for Gladys Betteridge, who was working for the soft furnishing shop of A & G Barnes in Lavant Street (now One Tree Books). The curtains were made of a heavy twill material and the blinds were dark green in colour.

It was 'Make do and Mend' time, and hand-me-downs and ingenious sartorial adaptations were the order of the day. Every family would routinely mend and darn clothes, visit shops which dealt in exchange or second-hand goods, and salvage anything which could be recycled in a new form. At Christmas time, for example, people could go to Jacobs and Hunt's auctions to find old bicycles or dolls' prams. At Adhurst Farm, where Norma Collins' father was stockman and cowman, rugs were fabricated out of farm sacks, washed clean and interwoven with strips of old clothing. Jenny Dandridge remembers having her shoes cut open at the front to accommodate foot growth. Frugality led to Vicky Ball's grandmother skinning rabbits, pegging the skins out on a board and rubbing salt and vinegar into them to cure and clean them, then cutting the fur into strips to place on the tops of boots to make them warmer in the cold winter months. The exigencies of war created their own tailoring styles: Karin Antonini, for example, remembers the thrill of being fitted for a dark brown siren suit to wear over her pyjamas when the pupils at Bedales had to head for the school trenches at night!

Coupon-swapping became a common occurrence. Shirley George exchanged her sweet coupons for her neighbour's clothing coupons: in this way she preserved her teeth and gained a coat! People had necessarily to adapt to the prevailing conditions: women wore ankle socks which required fewer coupons than stockings. Queuing was both a nightmare and a blessing: in the queue some fruitful bartering often took place as people found the opportunity to bargain with others for goods they were seeking. In such conditions it was also inevitable that a limited black market sprang up. By all accounts, however, this was not widespread in Petersfield, as most people had access to friends or relatives who could offer them free or exchange goods, or they knew shopkeepers who occasionally had 'a little bit extra' that week. Mrs Rotherham, for example, whose husband was a small-time farmer, could offer butter or eggs in her little shop in College Street.

Of course, petrol rationing also had its effect on everyone's lives. Anyone who gave lifts to others on a regular basis was entitled to an extra allowance of petrol. As a result some folks brought their horses and buggies to get about the town. Others walked or cycled for miles to get to and from work, while others had gas-driven cars (with gas bags on top). Of course, it was relatively rare for families to own a car until the 1950s, and in the country as a whole there were only about two million cars in 1939 (although there were also half a million motorcycles). In Petersfield it seemed that all the cars were of pre-war vintage, taxis drove along at about 12mph, and crossing the road merely involved avoiding the occasional handcart or horse-drawn delivery vehicle. Sixty years later, at the turn of the twenty-first century, there were ten times the number of cars on the roads and Petersfield is now benefiting from its own bypass.

MYSTERIOUS EVENTS

A mysterious story appeared in the *Squeaker* in late August 1941 about an 'Austrian alien', who was reported to have spent one night at the Commercial Hotel (the building next to St Peter's church now occupied by the solicitors Macdonald, Oates), run by Mrs White. Some people also recall the story of a 'spy' in the area, although this may well have been the natural exaggeration of fear playing tricks on the heightened imagination of local people in wartime Petersfield!

At the Harlequin café in Sheet Mrs Hilda Barnes recalled a man who had come into the café during the war and given her so many different accounts of his postings that she reported him to the police. He was later discovered to be a spy.

And then there was the story of a female spy at the Home from Home canteen . . . or was that merely a fear induced by the very obvious potential for eavesdropping on the military at such an open establishment?

Shirley George remembers going into a wood in Steep with some friends and spotting a case – which they couldn't open – pushed under a bush. So they went back home to fetch her father's tools, but when they returned the case had gone. They realised that someone had been watching them. . . . According to Shirley, there was always an air of mystery ('funny goings on') near the Bedales estate, which she believed was linked to the presence of conscientious objectors in the area.

Secrecy is part and parcel of any wartime activity, of course, and what exactly was happening on Butser Hill remained clouded in mystery for most of the population of Petersfield. Vicky Ball's maternal grandmother, Helen Luker, was born a Seward, the farming family from Weston. Among her hobbies was painting and one day during the war she caught a bus to go and paint Butser Hill. She sat beside the road with her easel, painted away for a few hours, then returned home to 22 High Street, Petersfield. Early that evening there was a ring at the front door and a policeman asked to be let in. To her surprise he wanted to see her painting, and he appeared very relieved when he saw that she had not drawn any construction on the summit of the hill. It seems that old Mrs Luker had been observed sitting below Butser and was thought to have been taking down notes about the lookout station at the top. The observer may even have considered her to be a spy, dressed as an old woman for this purpose!

The rubber 'Minibrix' – as the name suggests, a precursor to the children's toy of the plastics age, Lego – which had been manufactured at the Itshide factory in Sandringham Road under the trade name of Premo, ceased production in 1942. Contemporary rumour had it that munitions were being manufactured there.

In fact, for the next five years the factory concentrated on rubber products for the Ministry of Defence: tank treads, instrument suspension, rubber soles for commando boots and various medical items. Output from the Itshide (ITS Rubber Ltd) factory could be loaded directly on to a train by virtue of having its own siding adjacent to the Midhurst branch line; the factory eventually closed in 1987.

And what of Stocklands stables and riding school in Sheet? Firewatchers there reported that they were never allowed inside the building and that a rumour was spreading about a spare aircraft being housed there in the event of an emergency! In addition to this piece of contemporary gossip, Gwen Collinson Stokes remembers a man from the Ministry of Aircraft Production inspecting them on 1 April 1943 (and he was no April Fool!). However, it emerged later that, when Mr and Mrs Clark, who had started the riding school in 1936 vacated the property and went to Wales in 1940, the Air Force had requisitioned the stables as a shelter for sixteen dismantled Spitfires after an aircraft factory near Southampton had been bombed.

What the Itshide factory and Stocklands stables examples show is that it was perfectly possible for war-related production to take place without local people themselves being aware of it. Even if they had come across something strange, they remembered the motto 'Walls have ears!' and supposedly clandestine activities could continue to flourish.

THE BELL HILL MANUFACTURING COMPANY

One factory which was certainly running a clandestine operation was the Bell Hill Manufacturing Company, owned by Frank Jones. He was a master cabinet-maker who had had his own furniture design, manufacturing and retailing business in Southsea in the 1930s, and had won a contract to supply all types of furniture to naval establishments in the south of England. His wife worked closely with him and looked after the accounts for the business; his daughter Madeleine (now Madeleine Walker) also helped out in the office during her school holidays, as well as learning soldering and welding with other girls in the factory in her early teens. The family had also acquired a holiday cottage in West Meon. When war broke out, the work of furniture-making evolved to become a (clandestine) manufacturing base for aircraft parts; however, the factory was demolished by an incendiary bomb during the blitz on Portsmouth in January 1941, which set the cellulose in the workshop alight. Madeleine remembers seeing the aftermath of the fire: the building was gutted and there were 'icicles' of molten glass dripping down the outside of it. Frank Jones, desperate to fulfil his contracts, joined forces with Paynes of Bedhampton and began looking for new premises to carry out the war work. He eventually found Ruttles builders' yard in Petersfield, at the bottom of Bell Hill (now 39, 41 and 43 Bell Hill), which consisted of a two-roomed office block and a row of wooden sheds. They were still short of sufficient space for a factory, however, and so some mushroom sheds were purchased from Froxfield, which were dismantled and reconstructed on the Bell Hill site by the workforce in a matter of days. Machines for the factory were found from anywhere where they were no longer being used, and the manufacturing process was re-started from scratch. The original workforce from Portsmouth was supplemented by new recruits, in the form of directed labour, from London and elsewhere, totalling approximately fifty to sixty people, who were employed by the newly formed Bell Hill Manufacturing Company. The *Squeaker* began to carry adverts for accommodation for these incomers under the guise of 'accommodation for war workers', without specifying either the type of work or its whereabouts, all of which had to be kept secret. Frank Jones was now employing women in his factory for the first time; they had to work entirely separately from the men, with a women's manager appointed to direct them and to represent their interests. The work was then divided into a machine shop (male employees), followed by an assembly shop (female), then a spray shop (male).

Frank Jones had to go to London to the Ministry of Defence to receive instructions for the designs which he then had to submit for approval. The paperwork had to be kept under tight security in the family safe and Madeleine had to remain silent about the work and about the people she saw coming to the house. One of the contacts at the Ministry was a certain Major Denton who lived at Froxfield, who ordered the construction of flat rafts to be used by merchant vessels, with loops of tarred rope around the edges and the rope whipped at either end. This work was performed by outworkers in West Meon and the completed products became known as 'Denton floats'.

The most important and clandestine part of the operation was that concerning the all-wooden plane parts which were produced at the factory. The initial contract was for Airspeed Oxfords, but this was followed by parts for Mosquitoes (the new twin-engined light bombers which started production in 1942), and tail sections for Horsa gliders, for which Madeleine did the wiring. The factory also continued to make furniture for the Ministry of Defence. Part of the secrecy of the whole operation was dependent on the workforce not seeing a finished product – the fact that only parts were made, assembled and finished helped in this respect. The parts were then linked to other parts produced elsewhere in the country to complete the process of building planes for the Air Force in general and for the D-Day landings in particular.

ENTERTAINMENTS

On the musical front, Petersfield continued to offer a wide range of activities and entertainments. In January 1941 Dr Norman Newell organised a series of musical evenings at the Station Road Methodist church hall and he was also responsible for recruiting players and singers for a performance of Haydn's *Creation* in the Town Hall in March. In April 'the most sensational story in Petersfield's musical history' occurred when the London Philharmonic Orchestra played under the baton of Dr Malcolm Sargent, and the soloist in Beethoven's *First Piano Concerto* was Denis Matthews. With military correctness, he appeared in uniform on stage and was identified in the programme as 'Aircraftsman' Dennis Matthews. In May the 36th Petersfield Musical Festival was held and this lasted three days. Since the Town Hall was also the main base for Air Raid Precautions, the immediate need for an alternative use of the hall dictated that there should be no raised platform that year. It was Dr Newell, the Emanuel School music master, who instigated some choral singing by servicemen whom he recruited at Longmoor Camp.

Soldiers from New Zealand, who were based at Langrish, used to give tree-chopping exhibitions on the Heath in the summer, and they performed the same feats at Churcher's College Sports Days. In July 1941 the New Zealand Prime Minister, the Rt Hon. Peter Fraser, visited a forestry unit of the New Zealand Expeditionary Force, which for months had been felling trees in the Petersfield area.

The Taro Fair of 1941 was an improvement on the previous year's. The UDC decided to allow 'something in the shape of a fun fair' as a distraction from the strain of the war and this was clearly a highly popular move. Although the horse sale in the morning was relatively limited – nevertheless about sixty horses were sold at Hall, Pain and Foster's Show – the afternoon amusements lasted until blackout time and drew thousands of people. In those days one of the main attractions was the boxing booth, where volunteers could come and fight 'the champion'. June Brooks remembers with pride her uncle, Charles Anstey, actually defeating the man and winning a prize! After leaving the army Mr Anstey taught boxing at Churcher's College!

THE BRITISH RESTAURANT

In autumn 1941 an article appeared in the *Squeaker* about the success of British Restaurants throughout the country. These emergency feeding centres had first been mooted the previous winter owing to the problem of feeding thousands of Londoners rendered homeless, either by the bombing or by damage to gas and electricity mains. New communal restaurants were soon approved by the Ministry of Food, who paid the capital expenditure incurred, and these were later named British Restaurants, often occupying schools which had been evacuated and which were the easiest buildings to adapt. In less than a year over eight hundred had been established; they provided good, substantial meals of plain but well-cooked food, at prices ranging from about 8*d* to 1*s*. They were patronised not only by those who had lost their homes, but also by factory workers who had no canteen and for mothers too busily employed on war work to cook for their families.

A British Restaurant opened in Petersfield the following January. It was housed in two Nissen huts at the back of the Town Hall and provided a dining hall capable of accommodating 250 people at one sitting. The opening ceremony was presided over by Keith Gammon, the Chairman of Petersfield Urban District Council, whose strong initial support for the venture, together with the efforts of Miss Tomkins, Chairman of the Restaurant Committee, had ensured its arrival. Under the new manageress, Mrs Thomson, the restaurant served a midday meal between 12 noon and 2 p.m. and snacks between 10.30 a.m. and 4 p.m. It was intended that anyone could use the new facility, one of its advantages being that by cooking and feeding centrally, there would be a considerable saving in food and coal as well as in time and manpower. The staff of the restaurant numbered about twelve, and, like all other British Restaurants, it had to be financially self-sufficient.

From the moment of its opening in January 1942 there was a steady increase in the demand for meals: in the first four days alone, 1,489 meals were served; in the second week, 2,791; in the third week, 3,249. This settled into a pattern over the coming months, during which an average of 3,000 meals were served each week, clearly fulfilling a need in the town. By the summer up to 4,000 meals were being served per week, thus totally justifying its existence by providing a fine service to families, local shop and office workers and a small number of schoolchildren.

HOP-PICKING

In the late nineteenth century Vicky Ball's great-grandfather, William Seward, grew 'fuggles' – a high quality and very profitable strain of hops – at Weston. (They were also larger than the other types and so it did not take so long to pick a bushel.) The gathered hops used to be transported to the Hop Garden in London to be valued, and when there was a good yield Mr Seward would be met at home by his daughters in eager anticipation of their father who, having gone straight to Hatton Garden with his profits, would bring them each a piece of jewellery!

Until 1953, when disease attacked the vines, the extensive hopfields in Buriton and Weston were an important local industry and a source of employment for both Petersfielders and seasonal pickers from Portsmouth. To reach the topmost poles at the time of 'stringing', ladders were used at Buriton, but stilts at Weston. Harvesting was carried out in September and lasted for three or four weeks, and the money earned from this work was often used to buy footwear and clothes for the winter. School holidays were arranged to coincide with this period and children sometimes had an extra week off school to help; some of their hard-earned pocket money was spent at the Taro Fair (6 October), which generally marked the end of the hop-picking season.

The pickers from Portsmouth lived in huts on the site in Weston but, regrettably, these huts, which could be plainly seen from the railway and the main Portsmouth road, were completely destroyed by a fire in September 1941. At the time they were being used by about two hundred Portsmouth refugees who had been blitzed out of their homes in the recent raids. The forty huts had recently been requisitioned by the Ministry of Health with a view to improving them beyond the September deadline which had been set to demolish them. Plans had been drawn up to build new huts, a nursery school and a social centre at the site, but the foundations for these structures had now also been razed to the ground. Fortunately, the families themselves had all been away at the time, hop-picking in the Mapledurham area.

Hop-picking in Weston. (Author's Collection)

As a result of the fire many families were made homeless, and these people were given temporary accommodation in the Village Institute in Buriton; others found shelter in tents provided by the Society of Friends, which had been doing much for the welfare of the hop-pickers for several months.

Some of these families would have found accommodation in the fifty-two hop-pickers' huts which were located at Buriton, more commonly known as the Buriton Evacuation Camp as it housed many people, mainly docksiders, who had also lost their homes during the raids on Portsmouth. The conditions here at the outset were extremely crude and primitive, but the Rural District Council had subsequently improved facilities somewhat, including approving the provision of a recreation hut. An appeal was launched in the *Squeaker* for equipment for this amenity and a gramophone, a wireless set, books and handicraft materials had already been donated. Bedales School National Service Committee was also giving assistance by carrying out jobs around the camp.

HELP FROM CANADA

Canadian troops were based at Bramshott Common, on either side of the A3, in both world wars. In the First World War it was one of the largest training centres for Canadian troops in the UK and over three hundred Canadian troops, who succumbed either to the war or to the influenza outbreak of 1917–18, are buried in Bramshott churchyard. The Sunday closest to Canada's National Day, 1 July, is still marked by a service at the village church.

In the Second World War Canadian troops occupied two hutted camps and a hospital on Bramshott Common and were also stationed elsewhere, most notably at Bordon, which they virtually took over in 1940. Individual units of the Canadian Engineers were everywhere and they built workshops, camp roads, hospitals, railway sidings, and even a bypass and an airfield.

A raid on Dieppe in August 1942, with Canadians providing nearly 5,000 of the 6,000 troops involved, was a tragic disaster and the Canadians suffered 68 per cent casualties. In 1944 Bramshott Hospital received casualties from the Normandy invasion. The indestructible concrete floors of the hospitals and the maple trees along the A3 dual carriageway, planted in memory of the Canadian Forces, are now the only visible remains of these busy camps of the two world wars.

Children loved the Canadians; the Christmas parties laid on by them were great fun and the troops invariably showered the English children with sweets, chocolate and chewing-gum – a novelty at the time. There were even Canadian Father Christmases in the area. David Vincent and his friend Barry remember playing Cowboys and Indians in Petersfield Square one day before the fateful Dieppe raid and pinning a group of Canadians against a wall with their wooden tomahawks, demanding their surrender. The Canadians duly obliged and gave the children a couple of enormous Canadian apples for their pains. Whenever any Canadian troops staying at Katie Pitt's house received food parcels from home, they would contribute such luxuries as tinned chicken, tinned fruit or red apples to the family diet. On one occasion Clive Ellis, a 2nd Lieutenant in the Home Guard, needed a revolver, so his company commander bought one from a Canadian soldier for him! The Canadians also willingly traded their leather jerkins and other goods with Petersfielders.

Furthermore, a Canadian parcels scheme helped some child evacuees in the Petersfield district during the war. Two Toronto schools sent gift parcels regularly from the beginning of 1941; they consisted mainly of hand-knitted woollen clothes, knitted blankets (known as Afghans), and beautifully made baby clothes. Several classes from Clinton Street School in Toronto had a 'shower' for the evacuees – a collection of everything from 'soup to nuts'. There were socks, scarves, parkas, baby-clothes, handkerchiefs, toothbrushes, toothpowder and every kind of toilet necessity. Most of these goods went to Heath House, the sick children's hospital overlooking the Heath in Petersfield. Hughes School in Toronto also sent knitted gifts, including sweaters, blankets and socks. Several of the Canadian families 'adopted' Portsmouth blitz babies who were being cared for in a Petersfield children's home.

CHRISTMAS 1941

In keeping with the attempt to retain a feeling of normality in the town, Christmas 1941 offered everyone a fine fare of entertainment: apart from plays in the schools at the end of the autumn term (*The Rivals* by Emanuel School, *Twelfth Night* by Bedales), the Petersfield Choral Society put on Mendelssohn's *Elijah*, there was a pantomime in Sheet village hall, a grand carnival ball and three Christmas dances at the Town Hall, and a Christmas party for the troops at the Home from Home canteen which was attended by some three hundred service personnel.

It is evident that Petersfield suffered noticeably severe winters during the Second World War. It was common to see skaters in great numbers on Heath Pond and there were even attempts at makeshift games of ice hockey played by schoolchildren. For elderly people in particular the bitter cold weather brought hardships, with coal being rationed, efficient home heating almost non-existent and any water which may have been stored in bathtubs tending to freeze.

CHAPTER FOUR

1942

Troops in Town

EVENTS IN TOWN

The overall population of Petersfield and district had been increasing relatively rapidly: the estimated population in the Petersfield rural area had been 15,160 at the beginning of the war; by the end of 1941 it had risen to 23,300, not including members of the Armed Services stationed in the area.

The emergency maternity home, which had been operating at Collyers in The Spain since the beginning of the war, announced the arrival of its 300th baby in February 1942, and by the following summer this total had risen to 400. As for the numbers of evacuees in the Petersfield area, these were also rising: Sir Hugh Cocke's report on the government's evacuation scheme for 1941 showed a total of 2,833 billets in Petersfield (an increase of 1,330 over the previous year). There were also seventy-eight girls from Portsmouth High School boarding at Adhurst St Mary at this time.

'Warship Week' had been announced in February 1942, with a target of £120,000; a month later it had amassed £219,000. June Brooks' mother, Hilda Goode, was adept at attracting personalities from the musical and theatrical world to come to Petersfield during the war years: she managed to bring the pianists Arthur Rubinstein and Myra Hess to the Town Hall (they played on June's mother's piano borrowed from her house in Ramshill), and Joyce Grenfell the actress, all of whom performed free in full-length concerts. Don Brook's father also arranged for George Robey, the comedian, to attend another fund-raising event in Petersfield.

Perhaps the most interesting, and certainly the most popular, of these activities was a so-called 'Spotlight on Sappers' forces entertainment evening at the Town Hall on 6 February, when the RAF Symphony Orchestra gave a concert. However, it was the performance of Laurence Olivier which stole the show, and this report appeared the following week in the *Squeaker*:

> During the evening, Mr Laurence Olivier, the well-known and accomplished actor, wearing his uniform as an officer in the Fleet Air Force [*sic*], recited the fine, stimulating speech of Henry V to his troops on the eve of Agincourt and evoked enthusiastic cheering.

The same evening Olivier was called upon to deliver 'a singular and much applauded speech' about savings; and a hen's egg, autographed by Laurence Olivier, was later sold for 25s!

Laurence Olivier had, in fact, originally presented himself for service in the RAF during the war but, owing to a damaged nerve in his inner ear, he was refused entry

Petersfield's Naval Tradition

For generations Petersfield and the villages round it have contributed many men to the Royal Navy and we are proud of it. Now we are asked to help build more ships to hasten the day of victory. Every penny we can spare to lend to this Cause will help our own friends and relations who are hourly risking their lives for us. Let us not fail them.

Our target—
a Corvette,
£120,000
must be raised in
Petersfield
& District
WAR SHIP
WEEK

Sat. Feb. 28—Mar. 7

H.M.S. *Primula*

Advert in the Hants and Sussex News, Warship Week, 1942. (Hampshire Museums Service)

into a combat unit. Instead he joined the FAA (Fleet Air Arm) and found himself stationed at Worthy Down near Winchester. June Brooks remembers her mother driving Olivier back to his cottage at the end of the fund-raising evening. As they entered the hallway they were confronted by a full-length portrait of Vivien Leigh. Olivier said to the fourteen-year-old June: 'Don't you think that's the most beautiful woman you've ever seen?' to which she replied: 'Yes, and I'd like to be like her when I grow up!'

Olivier's most effective role in the war was without doubt in the field of propaganda, using his celebrity (and that of his new wife Vivien Leigh) and escaping the drudgery of his administrative posting with the FAA; in 1942 he was asked to play the title role in the radio version of *Henry V* that was being broadcast for morale purposes. With its stunning pageantry, its patriotic themes and its portrayal of the great English victory over France at Agincourt it was considered an ideal vehicle for such propaganda, and Olivier set about transferring it to film the following year.

HAMPSHIRE FARMERS & THE FOOD SITUATION

In April 1942 local producers and domestic and poultry farmers held a meeting to discuss the next winter's possible food shortages. The importance of keeping small stock was stressed, as this would ensure that gardens were properly manured; rabbits, chickens and pigs were also wanted and these could all be reared by individuals, thus reducing the need for Whitehall bureaucracy to dictate procedures. 'Good old household husbandry' was called for, and it was agreed that everyone should be encouraged to grow livestock or vegetables, or preferably both. It was pointed out that of Britain's 40 million population only about 7 per cent made their living from the land. Before the war the other 93 per cent had therefore been relying very largely on imported foodstuffs, but this must now change and it was the farmers' job to feed the people who lived in the towns and worked in the factories. This meant that country-dwellers should make it their duty to feed themselves. Immediately before the war agriculture had been a depressed industry: if one had travelled the 20 miles between Petersfield and Winchester, practically every other field on either side of the road would have been derelict, worn-out pasture, grazing no stock and producing nothing. Since the war had begun there had been a complete transformation, with the same farmers doing what they had always wanted to do – being allowed to farm their own farms and doing their job for the national interest at the same time.

Hampshire was one of the best-known arable counties in the country, but since 1939 Hampshire farmers had ploughed out of grass into arable more than one fifth of the whole county. The War Agricultural Executive Committee for Hampshire controlled many thousands of acres of land and over a hundred occupiers, who were generally too old to farm it themselves, had been prepared to give their land over to younger men. This whole operation was run by the farming community itself for the benefit of the country as a whole.

Farmers obtained some help with their labouring work from three sources: a small number of conscientious objectors, an equally small number of Land Army girls and, eventually, Italian and German prisoners of war. Peter Winscom employed all of these in Stroud, where the POWs were housed in Nissen huts by the village hall; the land-girls lived either at home or in hostels in the area, one of which was situated in a property in Heath Road.

People who were lucky enough to have their own back gardens had set about transforming their land into stock-keeping areas for rabbits, pigs, poultry and bees. Early in 1941 the government had begun to realise the importance of the production of tame rabbit meat, and in various areas, including south-east Hampshire, organisations had been set up to promote this work and to help householders with free advice and practical assistance.

SHOPS & SHOPPING

What characterised Petersfield more than anything else in the war years, indeed from the early 1930s until the late 1950s, was the proliferation of long-standing family firms whose individual shops and offices filled the three main commercial streets of the town, the High Street, Chapel Street and Lavant Street. Names now gone forever still stir happy memories among the older generations in Petersfield and the remarkable degree to which these residents are able to remember each individual shop suggests that their identities, whether highly respected, quirky, idiosyncratic or just plain notorious, were of paramount importance. Multiples simply do not arouse such affection, however well they are patronised.

A glance at Petersfield Area Historical Society's excellent monograph 'High Street Petersfield' gives a clear picture of the development of the ownership of the shops, banks and offices in the main thoroughfare. The National Westminster Bank, for example, is on a site which has been occupied by banks for nearly 200 years; likewise, Boot's occupies a plot which has been a chemist's for about 150 years; and Threshers' premises has been a wine merchant's for over a century. Of all the premises in the town dating from generations back, however, it is undoubtedly the pubs which have survived the longest, although their number has diminished considerably over the years. The one remaining private house in the High Street (at no. 22) is on the site of an inn, the Half Moon, while the site occupied by Winton House and Winsers was originally the White Hart Inn.

The Punch and Judy Restaurant, now ASK. (Petersfield Museum)

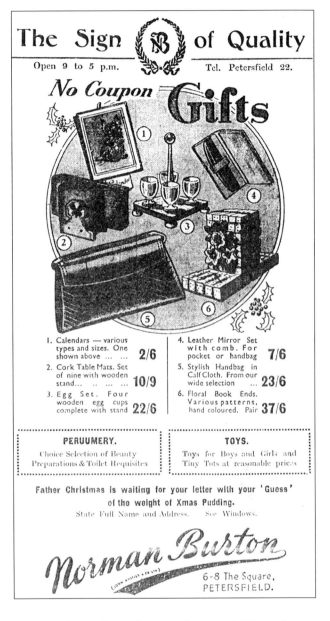

Norman Burton's advert in the Hants and Sussex News. *(Hampshire Museum Service)*

During the Second World War Boots and Woolworths, Barclays and Westminster Banks, the Co-op, Roland, Son and Vincent and the pubs in The Square all stood where they exist now, and the names (but not necessarily the ownership) of some shops have remained unchanged: Rowswells and Bassetts, for example, fall into this category. In his witty and comprehensive account *To School and Back: 1940s Petersfield*, David Scurfield has identified many of the favourite haunts of Petersfield shoppers: the seventeenth-century premises of the Punch and Judy restaurant (now ASK), beloved of the evacuees and their visiting parents, the late eighteenth-century Childs' concave glass-fronted printers and stationers and home of the *Squeaker* (demolished in 1964 and now Marks & Spencer), Flora Twort's arts and crafts and bookshop at 1 The Square (now regrettably split into three), Mrs Whitehead's Music Studio (now Your Move estate agents) serving schoolchildren with their '78s', entertaining the jazz enthusiasts of Emanuel School, and providing close-neighbour Mrs Money-Chappelle (and others) with her sheet music, instruments, books and records.

Before the advent of multiple, nationally generic shops Petersfield boasted Norman Burton's outfitters (now Heidi's and Carphone Warehouse), Edward Privett's the men's tailors and outfitters (now New Look), Pink's the grocers (now Constad jewellers), George Bailey's the greengrocer's (now Card Shop), Fuller's the grocers with their own bakery at the rear (now Petersfield Photographic), Mr Fielder's corn chandlery (now Liphook Valet Services), Gander's the butchers and fishmonger's (now Superdrug), who also had a second shop, a fruiterers and florists (now Cubitt & West), Wells and Rush the drapers (now Pizza Express), Whittington's Gents' outfitters (now Cardfair), International Stores (now Age of Elegance), and Forrest Stores (now Millets), all high-class establishments attracting large clienteles. In common with the Co-op, Fuller's sported the mechanically exotic, child-fascinating, commercially efficient wire-and-catapult system designed to get customers' money to and from counter and cashier. However, it was, inevitably but happily, the owners of the shops whose personalities remain in people's memories. Mr W.J. Fuller was an opulent-looking gentleman with dark suit, gold watch and fob, who bowed every customer into his shop; Mr Archibald T. Emm, who ran a

Pink's the grocers in the High Street, now Constad jewellers. (Petersfield Museum)

Fuller's the Grocer's advert. (Petersfield Museum)

china and glass shop in Lavant Street and was more known for his ill-fitting wig than for what he sold; Flora Twort, who greeted friends and newcomers with her charming smile; the pipe-smoking, waxed-moustachioed bicycling newsman Frank Carpenter; the charming staff (or were they moving dummies?) in Privett's window; the sweet, imaginative and ever-welcoming Kay Mace and Ena Hall of the Punch and Judy restaurant. It might not have escaped the notice nor the wit of visitors, too, that Petersfield boasted a butcher called Baker, another called Bone, a poulterer called Gander and an undertaker called Boxall!

Intriguing too, especially for children, were Fred Hind's junk shop (at the corner of Dragon Street and Sussex Road); S.P.Q.R. tobacco shop (with a Roman aroma?), the little bookshop at the top of Sheep Street – straight out of Dickens – and, opposite, George Money's furniture shop; the Handy Stores (now Bath Travel); the Barn run by the Gadstones; Joe Smith's forge; and Mrs Cosham's sweet shop in Lavant Street. Children's stomachs were readily satisfied with the hot rolls from Forrest Stores or Mr White's pies at Baker's and it wasn't long before the evacuees from London came to discover warm lardy-cakes which they bought at Fuller's. Of course the market provided entertainment in itself – to be able to touch the larger animals at close quarters in The Square or the smaller ones in the poultry market (where Waterlooville Carpets now stands) was a joy, even if the children were secretly willing them to escape!

A typical Lavant Street frontage in the 1930s and 1940s.

Lavant Street still had a partly residential feel to it during the war and examples of the remaining respectable Victorian middle-class houses, between which the shops were interspersed in the 1940s, can be glimpsed today behind the Help the Aged premises. Doctors and dentists were more centrally, and more individually, evident than the multiple surgeries of today, so often now situated further from the middle of the town: Dr Hugh Jeffries was at the eighteenth-century building at 15 High Street (now Present Surprise) and Charles Dickins the dentist in a grand early seventeenth-century white painted house with a hedge in front, known as Clare Cross (now part of Dolphin Court). When the wholesale demolition of many such properties struck in 1964, people wept for 'old' Petersfield. It was a cruel blow and, as David Scurfield has said, 'it was as if someone had decided to shake Petersfield out of its torpor'. It is hard to resist the conclusion that some of the architects' babies were thrown out with the developers' bathwater.

HMS *Primula*

The year 1942 marked the tenth anniversary of the sad loss of HMS *Petersfield*, wrecked while on service in China. As if to compensate for this loss the town of Petersfield was given the opportunity to sponsor another ship: this was the corvette

The old bookshop at the top of Sheep Street, now part of Macdonald, Oates. (Petersfield Museum)

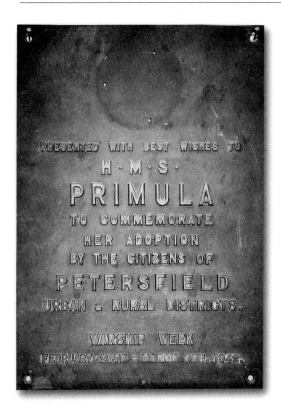

A plaque commemorating the adoption of HMS Primula. (Author's Collection)

HMS *Primula*. In a letter from the Admiralty in May that year it was announced with satisfaction that, as a result of the successful Warship Week campaign earlier, Petersfield had reached its financial objective and hence its entitlement to 'adopt' HMS *Primula*.

The *Primula* was a Flower Class Corvette, of which 145 were built during 1939 and 1940 to provide fast convoy escorts for the Atlantic run. Their short length (203ft) and shallow draught made them uncomfortable ships to live in and seasickness was a constant problem and a health hazard. The ratings on board were mostly reservists and the captains ex-Merchant Navy personnel.

A NEW CAMP AT WESTON

In September 1941 the fire which had accidentally begun in one of the hop-pickers' living quarters in Weston, and quickly spread to and destroyed all the adjoining huts, left destitute the Portsmouth families who used them every summer when they came to pick hops for local Petersfield breweries. The hop-pickers themselves had been temporarily relocated into tents and later into a hostel run by the Society of Friends War Relief Service (Quakers). During the winter of 1940/1 evacuees from Portsmouth had come to live in the huts and they were offered accommodation in the partially bombed workhouse building in Ramshill.

Out of the disaster, however, better conditions of life had evolved for the hop-pickers, thanks to the Society of Friends and the Ministry of Health who had devised a scheme for a permanent camp on Percy Seward's land not far from the old site at Weston. In July 1942 about a hundred people took possession of this new accommodation, adjoining Weston Lane, which consisted of several blocks of brick-built bungalows, together with a laundry, wash-house, shower-baths and a cookhouse for communal use. These new buildings had been planned by the local authority and the Society of Friends, the authority providing the cost of materials and some of the labour and a Quaker work party the rest.

THE URBAN DISTRICT COUNCIL

There was at this time a change of Chairman at the Urban District Council. Mr Keith Gammon, who had been Chairman of the UDC for the past three years, was succeeded by Mr George Bailey. The Rural District Council, meanwhile, elected Mr Charles Seward for a second three-year term of office as its Chairman.

At this depressingly low point of the war, with little optimism for the immediate future and an increasingly bleak outlook in the long-term, there was a good deal of debate on how to maintain morale in the town.

At their June meeting the UDC discussed the question of prosecutions against people refusing to take in evacuees, complaints from the public who had objected to iron railings being removed against their wishes, and the backlog of work involved in dealing with the thousands of premises whose exemption from fuel registration had been withdrawn. On a lighter note, an application had been received from Mr Meier, Headmaster of Bedales, for the free use of the Heath for a diversity of events, including a tennis tournament in connection with a school fête to be held at the end of June. The Recreation Grounds Committee agreed that the organisers should have a free hand, provided they clear up the Heath after the fête.

At the same meeting a request had been received for permission to shoot rooks on the Heath. This had been rejected. It was also reported that the Council had received an offer to sell them a set of manorial rent rolls and several other documents relating to the old Borough of Petersfield, for the sum of 8 guineas. These were documents dating from 1606, in the reign of James I, and extending to 1748. Miss Nora Tomkins, the Chairman of the Town Planning Committee, felt that if these were 'the piping times of peace' and they could possibly establish a municipal museum in which these things could be housed, they would be of interest. However, she feared that, as things stood, they would simply be kept in a safe, perhaps indefinitely. Mr Duffett stressed that this was an opportunity which would never recur, that they had ignored a very interesting document found in The Spain some years previously, and had 'let go' Castle House, a very historic building; feeling that the Council had been lax in that way, he offered half a guinea towards the cost of the documents. At the end of the debate the offer of the rolls was declined, with the Chairman remarking that it was open to any member of the Council to purchase the documents and make a present of them to the town.

Meanwhile, the previous year's order to remove railings and iron gates to supplement the national requirement for iron had been enforced. Except for railings that had been exempted on the grounds of public safety, the protection of cattle, or pending an appeal to a panel of architects because they possessed special artistic merit, all private or public railings had had to be removed. Impressively, a report now showed that the five counties comprising the southern region of Britain had provided no less than 11,000 tons of iron, nearly enough to construct one 35,000-ton battleship.

MUSICAL EVENTS

Despite the exacting circumstances of 1942, which the *Squeaker* referred to as 'times fraught with so much anxiety and stress as are these fateful days', the 37th Petersfield Musical Festival nevertheless managed to retain its uplifting power. It was a two-day event that year, with seventeen participating choirs, Sir Adrian Boult conducting, and, as had been the case the previous year, the absence of any competitive element or announcement of marks or order of merit for the choirs. In July the Town Hall was also the venue for a 'Children's Day', part of the Petersfield Musical Festival, to which 850 children came to sing, along with a string orchestra and a solo violinist, Marie Wilson, all conducted by Sir Adrian Boult.

Four further events took place that summer and autumn which greatly enriched the musical life of the town: in July the master pianist Mark Hambourg gave a recital in the Town Hall which attracted many hundreds of people, while the entire Wessex Philharmonic Orchestra made their first visit to Petersfield the same month, with Sir Malcolm Sargent specially engaged as their guest conductor. In October the London Symphony Orchestra gave two concerts in the town. The same month the Odessa-born world-famous pianist Benno Moiseiwitsch, who had settled in London and taken British nationality shortly before the war, gave a recital for the Aid to Russia Fund, the Red Cross and the St John Ambulance Appeal. Shortly after this Dr Norman Newell hosted a course of lectures for the WEA (Workers' Educational Association) entitled 'The Historical Development of Music'.

Music was undoubtedly alive and well in those dark days of 1942. Dr Newell's contribution to music, both at Emanuel School and also more widely in Petersfield, was significant; furthermore, two other Emanuel pupils, Ken Rogers and David Cameron, started to foster a love of traditional jazz in their pupils from 1942 onwards. The two pupils were billeted in Shackleford House in Dragon Street; this was the residence of Dr Robert Cross during the war, but after he had joined the Navy it was occupied by his two middle-aged spinster sisters, whom Roy Maxwell describes as 'the most incredible, lively characters'. Many Emanuel boys used to come to the house to listen to jazz records, purchased at the very popular Music Studio run by Mrs Whitehead (now the estate agents Your Move) and played on a wind-up portable gramophone. After raising money by auctioning his record collection one fine summer evening on Music Hill on the Heath, Mr Rogers bought a clarinet and began the formation of an embryo jazz band which rehearsed in the Methodist hall in Windsor Road. The schoolboy band 'Windsor Rhythm Kings' was thus born and it continued for the rest of the war, culminating in a spontaneous concert on VE Day in Petersfield Square.

'Jobs for Women with Brains'

A remarkable, and by today's standards of gender equality, inconceivably sexist entitled report 'Jobs for women with brains' appeared in the *Squeaker* of 3 March. Despite its overtly discriminatory tenor, it does reflect the wartime desire and willingness of many women to contribute simultaneously to the war effort and to their family incomes by taking on jobs in many different fields. The subtitle of the article, 'Good Housewives Make Good Candidates', seems by today's standards brutally patronising to women, but was at the time no more than the expression of a means of recruitment. As if to acknowledge the outright tendentiousness of the subject-matter, the article continued:

'Going into a factory' is a phrase on many women's lips in these days, and probably most of those who speak it have a similar picture in mind – a picture of manual work at a bench or machine. But factory work includes, in addition, many jobs that are a matter of interesting brain work and demand special aptitude for mechanical and mathematical interests.

What it is important to recognise here is that many pupils (girls, especially) left school at fourteen (the official school leaving age) without specific job training, or at sixteen with only their School Certificate. With these women in mind, the government set up a Women's Technical Services Register under the Ministry of Labour and National Service to cater for girls with credits in mathematics or science, to train them for jobs in industry. Many firms trained women in their own factories and training courses were laid on for those who were keen to become draughtsmen, assistants in planning, production and progress departments, in mechanical testing and metallurgical departments or estimating and rate-fixing offices; others became time-and-motion study workers, engine testers or electrical technicians and testers, while yet others went into laboratories as assistants.

Schoolchildren's Lives

It might be argued that, for various reasons, both the children of Petersfield and their evacuee counterparts who found themselves in the town were among the least concerned about the war going on around them. First and foremost, as children, they were less preoccupied than their elders by the constraints on their personal lives. Their education, although disrupted, was by no means unfulfilling – indeed, many of the activities they found themselves performing were positively beneficial to them as young adults and provided many opportunities to discover self-reliance, a freedom they could not have enjoyed in urban areas, and which even enhanced their feelings of altruism. Many men, schoolboys of the time, have said how exciting, even exhilarating, the war was for them, with its equal emphasis on the physical (helping with the harvests, for example) and pedagogical (academic education concentrated into half-days at school). The youngsters, unconsciously maturing at a rate far greater than either their predecessors or their successors, may well have benefited from the conditions they were being forced to live in and which prepared them well for the trials of adulthood, despite the obvious moments of tragedy which befell some of them. It is clear, too, that Petersfield provided a safe haven for them to grow up in and, indeed, to make friends in – friendships which were to last for the rest of their lives. Gladys Betteridge, for example, had a wonderfully helpful fourteen-year-old evacuee named Betty Dickinson, from Battersea Central School, who became almost a daughter to her – she looked after Gladys's young son, helped in the house, and kept Gladys company while her husband was working long hours as a baker and confectioner at Bishop's in Chapel Street. After Betty left school she worked in Petersfield until 1946, then became a GI bride and went over to America with her husband, but continued to write to Gladys weekly for many years afterwards.

In the summer of 1942 Battersea Central School opened its doors at Hylton House in The Spain (later Moreton House) to give visitors a chance to see the girls engaged in the everyday work of the school. It was described as 'an altogether gratifying and varied demonstration in the classrooms, kitchen and garden'. More importantly, perhaps, it was clear that here was a school providing everything that pupils could

Wartime fundraising with musical support. (Petersfield Museum)

wish for in educational terms, despite the outside world's encroachment on the lives of their parents. Mr Norman Burton's speech on behalf of the visitors talked of the magnificent training the girls were receiving in Petersfield under such ideal conditions, and the expectation that they would take with them pleasant memories of the town and the happiness they had enjoyed with its people.

It was not only during school terms that there was constant activity for pupils: in the summer holiday twenty-three Emanuel boys, aged between fifteen and sixteen and members of their Junior Training Corps, marched, with full equipment and with Major Hill at their head, from Petersfield to London (in other words, from Churcher's to their school at Battersea Rise) – all in the good time of thirty-two hours, this including a night spent at an army camp en route. The school's JTC adopted such route marches as a hobby and created set standard-distance marches for different age groups. As an example of the kind of fitness and commitment they achieved, two fourteen-year-old boys spent their half-term one year marching to Winchester and back – in a time of just under thirteen hours. Some of these energetic members of the JTC also took part in night treks and assault courses (constructed on a piece of land lent by Mr Keith Gammon, the ex-Chairman of the Urban District Council).

Schoolchildren also played their part in fund-raising activities. In July 1942 'The Schools Fête' was held at the Town Hall and on the Heath for the Relief of War Distress charity. Pupils from Bedales, Churcher's, Emanuel, Portsmouth High, Steep School and West Mark Camp organised amusements, competitions and games and attracted thousands of people. The great diversity of stalls included Bedales flower stall, Churcher's wooden and soft toys, West Mark Camp's craftwork, Emanuel and Churcher's copperwork, and Steep School's needlework. A grand total of £200 was raised for the charity.

Some measure of the logistical and educational difficulties facing the evacuees can be gathered from the report of the Petersfield County High School Speech Day of 1942: the school had increased its numbers to 180, working in six separate buildings in different parts of the town, and was still in need of another classroom for thirty-six girls.

THE TARO FAIR

The Taro Fair that same year attracted hundreds of people and consisted of a horse sale and a funfair. The Horse Show had been suspended until the end of the war. Although it did not approach the scale and variety of the pre-war fairs and it had to close down at blackout time, the funfair did provide a switchback, dodgems, a 'chairoplane', a children's merry-go-round, numerous try-your-luck stalls, and a variety of games such as darts and skittles. However, there were no cake or sweet stalls, no swing-boats, no coconut shies or shooting galleries. Messrs Hall, Pain and Foster conducted their usual Sale of Horses, and about seventy-five horses were sold, an increase on the previous year. This took place on the 'horsepiece', a section of the Heath adjoining Heath Road East. In the 1940s the Taro Fair was far larger than it is today: it stretched from a point opposite the end of The Avenue, alongside Heath Road, and almost as far as the cricket ground. The last horse sale took place in 1953.

THE HOME FROM HOME CANTEEN

In September 1942 the Home from Home canteen celebrated the first anniversary of its opening. Kathleen Money-Chapelle, the Honorary Organiser, reported that since its inception the canteen had provided over 300,000 meals and the average number of men served weekly was between 8,000 and 9,000. She had raised over £2,500 in the first year, only a few hundred pounds short of the target needed to repay the construction costs she had incurred. The activities of the canteen, apart from the meals it served, included Sunday night concerts, dances and dance classes; other facilities provided were games, a library, and a mending circle. The Home from Home had clearly been as successful as had been hoped by Lord Horder, whose full support Mrs Money-Chapelle had enjoyed, in providing food and entertainment for all servicemen and women on convoy work between London and the south coast.

A volunteer in the Home from Home Bookshop, which was established in 1941. It also ran a lending library and offered a service mending military uniforms. (Money-Chappelle Collection)

CHAPTER FIVE

1943

Debating the Town's Future

THE FUTURE CHARACTER OF PETERSFIELD

Perhaps surprisingly at this eventful and uncertain juncture of the war, questions were already being asked in the press about Petersfield's postwar future, a discussion which was to have repercussions for some time afterwards, both within the Urban District Council and for the general public. An article appeared in the *Squeaker* in January which recounted the details of a debate which had taken place at that month's UDC meeting as a result of an interview by the Town Clerk with a representative from the Ministry of Works and Planning. A question had been raised about industrial development in the town, to which the Town Planning Committee (under its Chairman, Miss Nora Tomkins) had replied that the Council were of the opinion that industries should not be established in Petersfield, the reason being that the natural beauty of the surroundings made the place especially suitable for residential purposes. The Committee felt that the character of Petersfield should be preserved as a place which would still remain a country town when, perhaps, others had become more or less industrialised. While there was no question of closing down the small industries currently in the town, such as the breweries, Miss Tomkins said that it would be 'a thousand pities' if Petersfield were to become 'just an ordinary little industrial town', wiping out the very qualities which attracted people to it. She thought that one of the most disastrous things that could happen would be if local people were to fail to preserve what was of value. She called upon the committee to take some steps themselves which would pre-empt any moves by an anonymous committee within central government to define Petersfield solely as a beauty spot and thereby preclude any scope for even light industrial development, thus changing its nature irrevocably.

Mr G.R. Jolliffe believed that the ratepayers should have some say in the matter, while Mr N.R. Palmer referred to Letchworth as a place built by people for retirement, but where, of their own free will, the residents had happily allocated a large area of the town to the building of factories. Mr Duffett stated that their object was to keep Petersfield both as a residential area and a beauty spot. The outcome of this debate was that the matter should be adjourned for another month to allow the public to have its say and for members of the Council to give it further consideration.

The following week, the *Squeaker* carried several letters from contributors: one expressed the view that it was their duty to hand down to future generations as much as possible of the beauty they had inherited; another accused the Urban District Council of hesitating on this issue when it should be fighting for the rejection of any industry in the town; yet another congratulated local builders, such as Pocock, Gammon, Holder, Woods and Mould, who had known how to locate 'multiple banks of cottages' like those in Charles Street with tact and without impacting on the 'residential type' of houses elsewhere in the town.

The February meeting of the Urban District Council pursued the discussion further. Present at this meeting were four representatives of the Petersfield Arts and Crafts Society, who expressed their view that any future building in the town should not interfere with the existing attractions or the natural beauty of the surroundings and that factories and the houses needed for the workers in them should only be built with the approval and sanction of a panel of qualified judges, specially constituted for the purpose. Opening the debate, Mr Alan Hinxman reminded the Council that there were 53 acres set apart in the town for industrial purposes and, given the future employment needs of those eventually returning from the war, this area could be extended for light industry. Mr Jolliffe remarked that a considerable proportion of the councillors had been appointed, and not elected, to serve through the war and that they were therefore not representative of the ratepayers themselves; he would be asking for a referendum in the town before the Council came to a decision on the issue. Mr C.E. Anstey felt that the town should accept some light industries. Mr S. Filer wanted to see Petersfield retain its character as a market town and residential area but, at the same time, thought there was plenty of room in the urban district for some suitable factories to be tucked away without intruding on any beauty spots. If five or six hundred extra people were employed, extra money would be spent in the town and he thought the commercial interests were entitled to have some consideration. The meeting concluded with the generally accepted feeling that some light industry could be acceptable, indeed beneficial, to the town, but that the question of zoning it in suitable areas was all-important.

THE EVACUATION SITUATION

In his report on evacuation covering the year 1942 Sir Hugh Cocke stated that the year had been a quiet one; there had been a steady drift back to the towns and there had been a fair amount of debilleting of those no longer eligible to remain within the scheme, although some of these had become residents of Petersfield. The estimated population of the Petersfield Rural District area was 21,041, compared with 23,229 at the beginning of the year, and 15,160 at the beginning of the war.

The number of unaccompanied children (children evacuated without their parents) had also decreased, from 395 to 325 over the course of 1942, excluding the 70 girls housed at Adhurst St Mary. Of the 943 accompanied children and their 1,223 accompanying adults in the town a year earlier, 500 children and 711 adults remained.

Sir Hugh mentioned that, although there was more room for evacuees than there had been in 1941, it could not be said that satisfactory billets were now easier to obtain, partly because more women were being called up and partly because suitable householders with both the time and the ability to take in evacuees were few and far between.

Within the Urban District Council area Mr A.P. Wilkins, the Chief Billeting Officer, reported a slight drop in the population (now roughly eight thousand) and this had relieved some serious overcrowding in many houses in the town. Despite this, he stated that the town itself remained very busy, as both a considerable number of unaccompanied schoolchildren as well as whole families expected to be billeted there, apparently appreciating the local amenities such as the cinema, the British Restaurant, the fish and chip shops, Woolworths and so on, none of which was available in villages. There was also a high number of war workers who used Petersfield as a dormitory town, travelling to Portsmouth on the early train and returning again in the evening. These people were officially registered as belonging to the population of Portsmouth.

THE WOMEN'S LAND ARMY

Soon after the start of the war Colonel Baxendale of Froxfield Green had written to the *Squeaker* praising the quality of his Women's Land Army volunteer, who had come from her civilian employment (as a manicurist) to work with sheep and cattle. The importance of the work done by these women in the Petersfield area was recognised by the award of badges to mark periods of service from six months to two years. At a gathering in August 1943 Mrs Alan Lubbock, who employed land-girls, paid a sympathetic tribute to them for the invaluable help they gave to local farmers. Acknowledging that their work was often dull and unspectacular, she reminded them that it was still a vital part of the war effort; she believed that there were many people who were 'country-blind' and did not see the natural beauty around them, but the Land Army could give them an opportunity to find out all sorts of fascinating details about country life.

A member of the Women's Institute claims to have 'grown up' in the Land Army. She was seventeen in 1943 when she first joined, and remained for three years, living in a hostel by the Heath Pond with twenty other girls and working on various farms in the area. According to the season they helped with hoeing, threshing, haymaking, harvesting, planting cabbages or sorting, sizing and bagging potatoes. In the evenings they would repair to the Home from Home canteen or the Town Hall to enjoy the dances and entertainments put on for the troops passing through the town.

The Women's Land Army not only fulfilled a labour need, therefore, but it also functioned usefully as a source of work for women in the country. It continued to operate after the war ended and was eventually disbanded in 1951.

In 1943 farmers were faced with having to increase their tillage area by a further million acres, in order to grow all the wheat and barley they possibly could for the nation's bread. Demands were made, too, for more potatoes, more feed and more dairy cows. The need for farm workers was to some extent satisfied by the employment of prisoners of war who were in the locality. Italian POWs were encamped at the top of Oaklands Road and they worked as farm labourers; others lived in a building by Stroud village hall and worked on Peter Winscom's farm. Geoff Paddock remembers them dressed in green, with a diamond motif on the back of their uniforms.

ENTERTAINMENTS

At the Savoy cinema in March *Mrs Miniver* was being shown. According to the press this was a screen masterpiece, which, as most people who had had the privilege of seeing it had agreed, was the most moving film of 'our finest hour', Churchill's phrase for the Battle of Britain victory of 1940. Starring Greer Garson and Walter Pidgeon, this Hollywood film, directed by William Wyler from a book by Jan Struther, depicted the bravery of British women coping in wartime. Indeed, women were noticeably the stronger characters. Kay Miniver, the eponymous heroine, captures a Nazi airman in her kitchen in a village near the south coast of England, and later her family huddles in their air-raid shelter as the house is partially wrecked by bombs. But it was the closing scene in a bomb-shattered church which stuck in people's memory and lent itself to a feeling of national pride: the vicar tells his congregation: 'This is the people's war. It is our war. We are the fighters. Fight it, then. Fight with all that is in us,' and V-formations of RAF Spitfires streaked across the sky as 'Onward Christian Soldiers' swelled on the soundtrack. Churchill claimed that *Mrs Miniver* was worth a fleet of destroyers in boosting Britain's cause, and the film won six Oscars in 1942.

The Petersfield Musical Festival of 1943 welcomed the participation of seventeen choirs, but it had to be limited to two days; naturally this was a disappointment to some, but the fact that it was even possible to continue a festival of this kind at all was a source of real satisfaction and mutual congratulation among all concerned. As the *Squeaker* noted: 'War conditions notwithstanding, this form of inspiration and relief from care, so much more needed in days of stress and strain than in peacetime, shall not lapse.' By special request Sir Adrian Boult, the distinguished festival conductor, kindly consented to hear the women's choirs individually sing selections from the programme they had prepared, and to comment on them. This was the first time Sir Adrian had officiated at the festival in such a capacity and, naturally, it was warmly appreciated by the audience.

Despite the privations of war families managed to entertain themselves as they had done before the war: children frequently set off on their bikes to the surrounding villages to see relations; in the summer they cycled as far as Hayling Island for family picnics; buses were frequent and reliable, and walking was as popular a form of relaxation as any. John Freeman enjoyed cycling with the Petersfield Cycling Club; Jenny Dandridge's mother belonged to the Women's League of Health and Beauty to keep fit; the radio was a popular form of entertainment at home. Families without a car could take the train to Havant and change on to the 'Hayling Billy' direct to the island, or they could take the Southdown bus which left Petersfield every half-hour to go to Southsea (a 2½-hour journey). June Brooks remembers the Steep socials at the village hall, organised by the daughters of Mr Grimshaw, the landlord of the Cricketers. Boys and girls met there for music-making, playing records and dancing; girls could also go riding on the ponies kept by Mr Grimshaw.

IN THE SCHOOLS

At the third anniversary of the West Mark Camp School the Warden, Mr W.J. Hawkins said that one good thing the war had done was to bring into being schools such as his. West Mark had also given many children an opportunity to live in a residential school for the first time in their lives. The worst incident of the war for them came one day in January 1943 when a lone German plane headed towards the building. The children were in the dining hall when a red (maximum) alert sounded; they left for the shelters at the rear of their dormitories but, just as they had covered about half the distance, the aircraft dived at them and unleashed a spray of machine-gun fire. Josephine Gillmore actually saw the pilot as she threw herself to the ground, then one bullet hit a boy in the knee, a small handful of children and the Camp Manager were injured by flying wood-splinters from a building, and some bullets lodged in the walls of the teacher's room at the end of one of the dormitories. As with the workhouse bombing, the pilot may well have mistaken the camp for an army establishment and decided to target the site; fortunately, no one was killed at West Mark, either then or at any other time during the war.

That summer approval was given by the County Education Authority for a youth centre in Petersfield, whose aim was to provide a room for members of local youth movements to meet for social and other activities not already included in their training programmes. The membership was open to all boys and girls between the ages of fourteen and twenty. Accommodation was provided at the back of the Senior School in St Peter's Road. The managing committee foresaw the provision of large, well-equipped rooms where the postwar plans for education were to be set in motion. Such plans were already under discussion by the government, who would publish them in R.A. Butler's Education Act of 1944. The youth centre was already open two months later and a report on its success in October 1943 showed that it was well supported, with its 173 members using the space available for discussions, dancing lessons, drama and boxing groups.

At an evening entertainment in the Town Hall at the end of the school year in early August Mr C.G.M. Broom, Headmaster of Emanuel School, expressed his gratitude for the hospitality which Emanuel pupils had enjoyed in the town. The host families had mothered and fathered them so extraordinarily well that he felt bound to take whatever opportunity he could to say publicly how grateful they all were, and to hope that on their return in September the townsfolk would continue their magnificent work and make the newcomers as happy as the passing guests had been.

At Battersea Central School's Open Day the same month the view was also expressed that the school had formed an integral part of the life of the town since the beginning of the war and many girls were now enjoying its educational benefits. With the new intake in September there would be nearly 200 pupils from Battersea in Petersfield. The school used Hylton House as its headquarters; the work of several classes was on display in the building and the pupils' horticultural skills were on show in the garden. Like other schoolchildren in the town the Battersea girls used the Methodist hall for their drama, dancing and singing, while the Senior School provided them with a domestic centre for their cookery classes.

When the new school year began in September Churcher's registered a record 365 pupils, including 111 boarders; this represented practically a tripling of numbers from sixteen years previously when Mr Hoggarth had been appointed Headmaster. Meanwhile, at the Girls' County High School there were 194 pupils.

DR GILBERT MURRAY

September 1943 saw the capitulation of Italy and this historic date coincided with the fourth anniversary of the outbreak of war in Europe. In Petersfield, as elsewhere in the country, the town observed the National Day of Thanksgiving. The same month the philosopher Gilbert Murray came to the town to speak to the Petersfield and District League of Nations Union; more than any other man he embodied the spirit of this League (the forerunner of the United Nations). From 1908 to 1936 he had been Regius Professor of Greek at Oxford, and from 1923 to 1938 Chairman of the Executive Committee of the League; in 1941 he had received the Order of Merit in the New Year Honours list.

His meeting in the Town Hall drew a capacity audience, including a large contingent of young people. He spoke on international unity and the prevention of war; ironically perhaps, despite the aims of the League of Nations which had been to save the world from another war after the

experience of the First World War, and despite the collapse in faith in the League engendered by the present situation, many people were now turning to them for guidance on how to bring peace-loving nations together again to stop the aggression and to promote cooperation.

The reason for the failure of the League of Nations, he said, was disunity among its proponents, principally Great Britain, the United States and France. The internal, mainly party-political, quarrels between the major nations had allowed Germany to become ever stronger. Replying to a question about how to prevent Germany from starting a third war, Dr Murray emphasised the need for her to be kept disarmed, yet, at the same time, be given the chance to recover her self-respect as a great nation. He believed that the easiest way to achieve this was for nations themselves to create a situation where the world might police itself.

THE HOME FRONT

During the summer the Royal Marines used the Heath Pond as a training ground for diving exercises. They lived in a tented camp by Sussex Road and constructed a scaffolding pier, jutting out from Music Hill into the water. Their divers barely reached the bottom of the Pond, but had heavy boots on to ensure that they sank easily.

In November volunteers were called for to make camouflage netting, which counted as a form of war service for those who were liable for conscription. This activity, which was coordinated by the WVS (Women's Voluntary Service), took place at the Drill Hall in Dragon Street. Netting was placed over a frame and coloured tape was threaded through the mesh; in his book, Norman Longmate quotes the WVS's historian who described this highly disagreeable, filthy task thus:

> the dust and fluff from the scrim half-choked the women knotting it on to the nets and the dye left their hands and clothes deeply stained. Crawling about with bruised knees and aching backs, elderly women drove themselves on for that extra hour which meant so many square feet of cover for the British Army.

At the Drill Hall in Petersfield, where Mrs Fellowes was in charge, some difficulty was caused by a gentleman who was colour blind and kept putting the wrong strips of materials on the patterns; Norma Collins remembers going along with other young teenagers to help interlace the khaki, brown and black strips into the netting strung up to the ceiling in the hall. They used to come home filthy from the dye which seeped from the material – but satisfied that they were doing their bit to help the war effort. In fact, probably unbeknown to those working on this arduous task, it was this netting which was used extensively to cover the tanks hiding in local woods before the D-Day landings, which were to take place six months later, in June 1944.

Two other forms of war work have been described by Mary Ray in her articles in the Petersfield Area Historical Society's bulletin: they are the grummets and the cable links produced for the Royal Navy. The first of these were strips of linen tape sewn round a metal eyelet, then detached from the metal 'former', the precise function of which remains unclear. Civilians – mainly women – were able to produce these articles at home. Mr Barnes, a garage owner from Harting, collected the finished articles in batches of 100 and sent them off to a naval establishment. The cable links were made under contract by Mr Suthers, who had an electrical and radio shop in Chapel Street; the workshops at the rear of his premises were transformed and his staff trained to produce these for use in naval radar. Supplies of cable and fittings would arrive for 'HMS *Suthers* – Petersfield' and, again, it was mostly young, female workers who did the 'war work' in this very local, and perhaps rather secretive, activity.

The work carried out by Miss Ida Henstock, an illuminator of manuscripts in her normal professional capacity, illustrates the kind of secret, and therefore very private, work which was being done by many individuals during the war.

KEEP IT UP!

THE "Glorious Few" who saved the world in 1940 have grown to a mighty host, shooting the enemy out of the sky in France, Africa and the Mediterranean. But more and more planes are needed to replace losses and strike at the enemy's heart.

We have engaged ourselves to provide 44 fighters costing £220,000. Our united efforts in street and village, in factory, shop and farm, and—not least—in school, will surely succeed. *But only the best from every man, woman and child will be good enough.* So—

Save and invest all you can in 15/- and 20/- Saving Certificates P.O. Savings bank - 3% Defence bonds 2½% Nat. War bonds - 3% Savings bonds

PETERSFIELD & DIST. WINGS *for* VICTORY

MAY 29th—JUNE 5th

Issued by the Petersfield and District National Savings Committee.

Advert in the Hants and Sussex News, *Wings for Victory Campaign, 1943. (Hampshire Museums Service)*

Miss Henstock spent the war at Bordean House in the drawing office of HMS *Excellent*, tracing and drawing gun parts for equipment manuals; later she produced drawings for the very secret new radar equipment, also for the Navy.

Despite the privations of the war many charities thrived at this time: a waste-paper recovery scheme got under way; Miss Vera Brittain made a national appeal for food to be sent to starving children in the occupied countries of Europe; the Aid to China campaign supported 'our allies in the Far East who battled against the common enemy'; and the Princess Tsahai Memorial Fund served to assist in the rehabilitation of Ethiopia (Princess Tsahai was the daughter of the Emperor Hailie Selassie).

Perhaps most impressive of all was Petersfield's contribution to the 'Wings for Victory' campaign, a national appeal for funds to pay for new aircraft, with Lord Horder as its President. In June 1943 the Petersfield branch of the campaign collected over £250,000, well over the anticipated target announced by Mr A.J.C. Mackarness, Petersfield UDC Chairman and Chairman of the campaign.

The all-prevalent and often traumatic war situation did not seem to diminish the enthusiasm for traditional entertainment in Petersfield – indeed, its presence probably enhanced the need for light relief. The October Heath Fair, for instance, which included the usual horse sale and fun fair, continued untroubled by events and attracted a crowd which even exceeded expectations.

The same month the *Squeaker* carried the astonishing announcement that a lion had escaped en route to Petersfield! This had naturally created much alarm and consternation at Clapham Junction, as the three-year-old animal had escaped from a boxcar conveying it from Wellingborough. The London papers, of course, gave some prominence to this story, the Southern Railway Home Guard were called out and, together with the police and others, followed the lion and confined it in a pit a few hundred yards from where it had escaped. Corrugated iron was placed around the pit to make a corral and Home Guards with loaded rifles stood by until the arrival of Frank Foster, ringmaster at Chessington Zoo, who took charge and succeeded in enticing the animal back into a crate. The lion was then transferred to another train and safely reached its destination; 'it seems quite a docile creature' the article ended.

To Petersfielders, however, accustomed as they were to the occasional grunting and roaring from Fred Kimber's menagerie on Tilmore Hill (whither the leonine Houdini was bound), the supposed drama was probably no more than another amusing incident in the life of Fred Kimber, one of the town's more colourful characters.

Another interesting character was Jim Daughtry, the rag-and-bone man who lived in a cottage in Swan Street next to the old hospital (and since demolished to make way for the new hospital). He traded in such items as scrap metal, rabbit skins, turnip tops, Victorian clothes from large houses, bric-a-brac and even primroses for re-sale. He had a long garden where he grew vegetables and fruit, a large shed to house the metal, rags and china he collected, and two stables for his horses and his cart. He also kept chickens at the end of the garden. His wife sold cottage flowers. Jim would sell rabbits for 1s, but refund 4d if customers brought the skins back.

FRED KIMBER

One of the most colourful characters of 'old' Petersfield was Fred Kimber, who, in his peaked cap and greatcoat summer and winter, sold newspapers outside The Square Brewery for nearly seventy years. But he was far more than a newspaper seller; by turn a billposter, newsagent, salvage collector, scrap metal dealer, footballer, animal dealer, property owner, euphonium player, bandsman and lion tamer, his multifarious business interests frequently induced something approaching apoplexy in members of the local authorities.

Born partially crippled in 1886, Fred had had to wear an iron support on one foot until the age of eight; this, however, did not stop him playing centre-half for Petersfield Town Football Club until the age of forty-five. As a euphonium player, he founded the town band in the early years of the twentieth century: it lasted for fifty years. Up to that time there had been several bands but none of them survived for long.

He lived in the end cottage in a modest row at the bottom of Tilmore Road, overlooking the railway line, and owned the land up to the top of the hill. But it was the cottage garden which attracted everyone's attention in more ways than one: one visitor to the property described it as

> like no other garden I had ever seen. Instead of flowers, little heaps of rusting metal sprouted all around. There were rows not of vegetables, but of piles of cardboard and scrap paper. Between the heaps and piles was a series of rather impromptu-looking cages – mostly boxes with chicken wire tacked on to the front – and at the end of the garden was a row of circus wagons and superannuated railway vans.

It was in these boxes and cages that Fred kept his ever-changing menagerie of animals, amazing, annoying and sometimes frightening many a neighbour and passer-by.

Indeed, his animals had perhaps the greatest impact on his life of all his trades: he claimed to be the first man in the country to hold a licence for training performing animals ('and you can

teach them without being cruel' he said). He bought, kept and sold all manner of animals, importing them for circuses and selling them on to road-shows or zoos. Taming a lion was as commonplace to him as keeping a pet donkey and he was reputed to have provided Chipperfields Circus with a wrestling bear.

His menagerie and circus paraphernalia would supply many a road-show before and during the war; he was as familiar with small animals – marmosets or coypus – as he was with lions, tigers and bears, and he was a natural magnet to birds or stray cats, wild or domesticated. His reputation spread far beyond the Petersfield area and trains were known to wait in Petersfield sidings (today visible but unused) to load animals for the Nottingham Goose Fair or a travelling zoo.

But newspapers were always Mr Kimber's first love. 'The little man with the big voice' was still selling papers in The Square until shortly before his death in 1970 at the age of eighty-five. Mr Kimber was eventually left a widower, but he had three sons, a daughter, and four grandchildren. Never having had much faith in written documents, Fred Kimber left no will, but one of his involuntary legacies would have made him grin: the estate of smart new houses built all over his sloping meadow at the top of Tilmore Road and labelled firmly KIMBERS.

Fred Kimber selling newspapers outside The Square Brewery. (Don Eades Collection)

CHRISTMAS 1943

That Christmas, the fourth at the Home from Home canteen, the servicemen and women were given a chance to enjoy some traditional entertainment: on 19 December there was a ceremonial stirring of the Christmas puddings in the centre of the main hall, accompanied by carol singing, and followed by an 'Odds and Ends' party in the evening. The hall looked exceptionally beautiful, decorated with coloured garlands, holly, and coloured lights everywhere. The atmosphere was warm, cheery and home-like, with log fires burning and a cheerful ambiance for the thousands of troops who came and went over the Christmas holiday period.

At the end of December, an article appeared in the *Squeaker* encouraging people to remain resolute in 1944, despite the continuing privations of the war:

Fred Kimber in his Tilmore Road yard. (Don Eades Collection)

It is a far cry from September 1939 to New Year's Day 1944. No one could have foretold on that sunny morning more than four years ago what course the next four years would take or what joys and sorrows were in store for us.

It is inevitable that after so long and difficult a period there should be times when we are weary and when it is tempting to relax our efforts. It is a remarkable tribute to our constancy of purpose that the stragglers should be so few, and that the will to victory of our people has remained unimpaired – nay, has even been strengthened – during these long years.

If we face 1944 with such a spirit of resolution, with a determination to make the whole war a personal triumph over our enemies, we can make it the decisive year in our history.

CHAPTER SIX

1944

The Beginning of the End

LIFTING SPIRITS

A certain dose of nostalgia crept into the correspondence columns of the *Squeaker* early in 1944. 'A.C.B.' wrote of his love for the town and its people recalled from pre-war days, when he had been one of the many boy assistants who had wheeled heavy loads on their hand trucks from the station to their employers' shops. His nostalgia for Petersfield stemmed from the fact that its citizens were, as he called them, 'home-grown'. He finished his letter by wishing the town 'and its whole composition' a Happy New Year.

In the next edition of the paper a soldier from Petersfield serving in Italy thanked the townsfolk for the comforts they had sent to the troops. His personal promise to bring victory sounded a little ambitious but perhaps not ill-founded, given his talk of the Germans falling back and his dream of exchanging cigarettes in Berlin with the Russian Allies.

The Headmaster of Churcher's College had also received a letter from a Petersfield man 'stationed somewhere on a gun site in the Middle East', thanking the school for sending a parcel of cigarettes.

In the town there had been a Grand Variety Concert at the Town Hall for three nights in January, featuring George Robey (the 'Prime Minister of Mirth'), with a supporting company including the Band of the Royal Canadian Ordnance Corps. On the same three evenings the Savoy cinema was showing the epic *The Life and Death of Colonel Blimp*, described as 'that magnificent piece of film-making' and starring Deborah Kerr, Anton Walbrook and Roger Livesey.

Of course little military information was, or could be, discussed by local newspapers at the time, but it was through such items as the above that a certain optimistic tone could be detected in people's thinking and nostalgia for their home town in their hearts. Despite the inevitable restrictions on press reporting, however, some pieces of news managed to get through: an airgraph from a 14th Army battery, originating from Petersfield and operating in Burma, was received at the *Squeaker's* offices. First, it briefly mentioned the boredom of relative inactivity for two years, then the more recent fighting in jungle conditions which, although hazardous, had been successful.

Two months later, in March, it was clear that plans were under way for an Allied landing somewhere in France. The press carried an announcement from the Secretary for War, who had issued orders making a considerable portion of Hampshire and the whole of the Isle of Wight 'Prohibited Areas'. The ban covered the coastal strip from the Wash round to Newquay in Cornwall. Petersfield rural district was also covered by the ban, which meant that anyone could be asked to justify their presence within the area. Unauthorised entry into such zones could lead to a fine or imprisonment and everyone over sixteen had to carry their identity cards at all times. It was forbidden to carry binoculars or telescopes.

NAVY NEWS

In January Captain C.H.L. Woodhouse, the Battle of the River Plate hero, was promoted to Rear-Admiral. Another Petersfield naval officer, Rear Admiral G.J.A. Miles, was promoted to Vice-Admiral. He was a navigation specialist and had commanded the battleship HMS *Nelson* from 1940 to 1942. Subsequently, from 1942 to 1943, he had become Head of the British Military Mission in Moscow. Another source of pride for local people was the award of the Victoria Cross to Lieutenant B.C.G. Place, DSO, RN, from East Meon, for his part in the most daring and successful attack on the German battleship *Tirpitz* on 22 September 1943. Lieutenant Place was the Commanding Officer of one of the Navy's two midget submarines which helped to sink the *Tirpitz* in Kaa fiord, northern Norway.

Meanwhile, Petersfield's adopted ship, HMS *Primula*, donated its battle ensign to the town in January and, after discussion in the Rural District Council about where it should be placed, it was agreed to hang it in the parish church.

NATIONAL & LOCAL RECONSTRUCTION

It was under the title 'National Reconstruction' that Dr Harry Roberts wrote a series of eight articles in the *Squeaker* in 1944. Dr Roberts was well known in Petersfield for his public services and he had been instrumental, along with Alan Lubbock, Mr A.J.C. Mackarness, Percy Burley, Dr Gabbatt, Miss Kathleen Merritt and Miss Marie Brahms, in raising funds for the construction of the new Town Hall, completed in 1935. His prime concerns were social problems and how to make the most of the land and the people of England, without any bias towards specific party-political views. He believed that the country had an industrial population suffering from insufficient wages, insecurity and bad housing conditions, and an educational system which fulfilled no real practical or moral purposes. He called for greater democracy and less bureaucracy, the elimination of poverty, and a more vocal and assertive political awareness on the part of the population. The two major problems of housing and education were those which required tackling first.

It was a good time to assess the postwar housing needs of the town, and at the Urban District Council meeting in April Miss Nora Tomkins outlined the government's proposals. A circular from the Ministry of Town and Country Planning made it clear that any housing development should be planned so as to fit into a neighbourhood unit, complete with all its necessary community buildings such as schools, churches, shops and so on. At the same time the so-called Grange site (by the Causeway) was brought into the picture because local authorities were now able to buy land for housing in advance and, given that this area had grown into quite a considerable neighbourhood, it was a site which the County Council could buy under compulsory purchase orders. By September the compulsory purchase of the Grange and Cranford Road site was complete: it was deemed 'a good plan with a gracious layout'; approximately 200 houses were proposed to be built on the 27-acre site.

A letter had also been received by the Council from the County Land Officer in May, indicating the desire to reserve a site for compulsory purchase on the south of Love Lane, opposite Churcher's, for educational purposes.

In the same month the Urban District Council discussed future educational facilities and developments in Petersfield. The 18 acres earmarked on the Love Lane site would, in Miss Tomkins' view, be best used for the construction of an educational block, rather than occasional buildings scattered around the town. Since everyone was aware that the erection of a new County High School for Girls was long overdue, this was the first item to be discussed. Mr Norton Palmer described the present building as 'not a proper place in which to teach children'. The structure was unsound, it had no proper light or ventilation and it was woefully overcrowded. Mrs Alan Lubbock put forward her view that educational provision in the town should be for all ages, from nursery school to college, preferably on one site, comprising 'a really noble group of buildings'. At the end of the debate the Council agreed to point out to the County Council the desirability of forming a complete education block on ground to be reserved for the purpose. It was known at the time that the Grange site had also been earmarked for elementary education. At the same meeting it was announced that an application had been received for Hylton House to be used after the war as a school for children from the ages of five to fourteen. The Council agreed to an amendment to the Town Planning map, whereby the planned use for Hylton House as a residential area should now permit it to be used for 'residential or school purposes'. Hence began the sixty-year history of the house as a school.

M. Roland Pullen wrote an article in the *Squeaker* in May about the inadequacy of the two major highways through Petersfield, the A3 and the A272, with the congestion caused by the level-crossing at the western exit to the town. His suggestion of a bypass seems now to have been a far-sighted one, although his proposal for a road passing to the east of the town would eventually be overruled by later councils and government. However, his visionary plan, based upon the belief that the town would have to contemplate an intensification of traffic after the war, together with a desire for greater accessibility from the coast to London and the advent of speedy motor transport for everybody, was well founded.

An appreciation of the town's architectural beauty was printed in another edition of the paper the same month; although tending towards the sentimental in its idyllic portrayal of the 'small, compact, well-planned, picturesque town' and its surroundings, its intention was clearly to forewarn the residents of Petersfield against future planners' building schemes, for fear they might destroy the town's rare qualities.

A letter to the *Squeaker* on 7 June, echoed King George VI's recent message to the nation ('I hope that throughout the present crisis of the liberation of Europe, there may be offered up earnest, continuous, and widespread prayer . . . whereby we can fortify the determination of our sailors, soldiers and airmen who go forth to set the captives free'): a mother, evacuated to Petersfield and living in Noreuil Road since her family home in Southsea had been wrecked by a bomb in 1940, called upon the mothers of Petersfield and of England to 'pray for these brave boys of ours, that we may gain a little of their indomitable courage'. She had been inspired by the sight, the previous night, of the mighty armada in the skies over Petersfield of planes and gliders heading for the French coast.

DR HARRY ROBERTS

Harry Roberts was born in 1871 in Somerset, trained as a doctor and set up his first practice in Cornwall in 1895. He met and married Jessie Groves and they had two children, Hazel and Denys. While in practice Harry began some freelance literary writing for the publishers Bodley Head, but he was also interested in the emerging socialism of the period and, as a consequence of his social and political interests, he moved to a medical practice in working-class Stepney in London's East End, where he formed the Stepney Labour League in the Mile End Road in 1907. A great philanthropist, he was often known as 'the sixpenny doctor'.

He supported the Fabian Society and, later, the suffragette movement, and his early pamphlets, such as 'Towards a National Policy' (1911) and 'Constructive Conservatism' (1913), were to colour a good deal of later social legislation. His reputation in the field of political writing began to matter as much to him as his career in medicine and, indeed, he was seen as a modern-day Cobbett. With his wife's antipathy towards living in the slums of London and Harry's desire to remain in practice in Stepney, the couple parted company and Harry remained in Stepney for over thirty years. Winifred Stamp moved in as Harry's housekeeper and companion, which she remained until his death at the end of the Second World War.

Harry launched himself into local politics and was in fact nominated as a prospective parlia-

mentary candidate for Stepney. However, the antics of some of his supporters, who were manipulating his very personal principles for their own political ends, drove him out of active politics for good and his centre of gravity gradually shifted from London's East End to Oakshott Hanger estate, which he had bought in 1909. The plot of 34 acres of woodland became his retreat from Stepney; it was here that most of his writing was done and where he remained for almost forty years. His obituary described him transforming the rough and wooded Hanger 'into a fertile and cultivated demesne of orchard, garden, wood and meadow'. He built some simple wooden huts there so that friends could visit at weekends; these huts were eventually also used as a sanatorium by some of his London patients suffering from tuberculosis. Winifred and a student friend, Marie Brahms (known as 'Bas'), moved in with him and a small coterie of friends slowly took shape. These included Geoffrey Lupton, a neighbour at the top of Oakshott Hanger, who built the hall and memorial library at Bedales School, Edward Thomas, the poet, Hester Wagstaff, an accomplished jeweller and a student of Winifred's, and Flora Twort, the portraitist. Margaret Penney remembers the group well: they would come down to Petersfield every day on horseback, tie their horses to the railings in The Square and sell their goods from the panniers they had loaded up at Oakshott.

THE PRE-D-DAY BUILD UP

Some of the Land Army girls who were living in Petersfield during the summer of 1944 remember finishing threshing a rick in a field by West Meon Hut crossroads when tanks began rolling down the roads from Alton and Winchester, heading towards Portsmouth or Southampton. They just sat on their sandwich tins, watching in amazement, knowing what it all signified. The next day they could hardly work for watching the extraordinary sight of hundreds of planes thundering past overhead, wing-tip to wing-tip, layer upon layer. On the Saturday of that week, when the land-girls turned up at Petersfield Town Hall for the regular dance, there were no men: Hampshire had been emptied!

One day towards the end of 1918, shocked at the impossibility of buying a serious book in Petersfield, Harry and Flora Twort decided there and then to purchase 1 The Square, which had fallen into disrepair. They restored it and rented it for twenty-eight years, thus creating a new cultural centre for Petersfield, which became an instant success. It was thanks to the shop that the Oakshott circle broadened its influence and into its orbit came the novelist Nevil Shute Norway and the artist Stanley Spencer.

Dr Harry Roberts was a household name in Stepney where his practice had become the largest private clinic in England. He continued to pursue his work there sporadically until, sadly, the clinic was bombed in 1941 and his life's work was shattered in a moment. By this time, however, he was beginning to suffer from a serious heart problem and was forbidden the smallest physical exertion. In Oakshott, his illness brought him into contact with Lord Horder, who described him as a man of two extremes, the contemplative and the iconoclastic.

Harry Roberts continued to write articles and reviews for the *Spectator* and the *New Statesman and Nation* among others; towards the end of the war, the series of articles on 'National Reconstruction' was first published in the *Squeaker*.

Perhaps his greatest contribution to Petersfield life was his championing of the Musical Festival and the Town Hall, both of which he helped to establish by personal intervention and benefaction; he organised the public appeal to fund the construction of the Town Hall and this project

subsequently received support from the Urban District Council. Shortly before his death he also pursued the idea of creating a public library in the Town Hall building. He was also active in Hawkley village life and started a youth club there.

Harry Roberts, doctor, writer, social reformer and 'champion of the underdog', died at Oakshott suddenly one November evening in 1946. A memorial to the man and his achievements hangs in Petersfield Festival Hall today.

Flora Twort's sketch of Harry Roberts.
(Hampshire Museums Service)

Flora Twort in her Church Path studio, 1954, with a sketch of Lord Horder. (Hampshire Museums Service)

An advert for the Petersfield Workshops from the 1938 town guide. (Author's Collection)

Lou Crosswell remembers the arrival of the Americans to erect telegraph poles along the main A3 road through Sheet – preparing the communications system for D-Day. They used strangely long American shovels to shift the shale and gravel which had been dumped alongside the road for the purpose, and crampons to shin up the poles.

Vic Walker's job on 3 June was to collect all the maps to be used by the Normandy invasion troops from Eisenhower's HQ in Southwick House, near Fareham. He left his driver at the Home from Home canteen and dropped in to see his family in Chapel Street on the way!

David Martin remembers picking his way to Churcher's through lines of tanks parked along the old A3 road. Roy Maxwell describes the passing tanks' effect on the hot tarmac as leaving the road surface 'like a frozen section of the Atlantic ocean in a storm'. Churcher's boys were asked not to bring bikes to school during those days: given the descriptions of the driving skill of some of the tank drivers, this was probably a good piece of safety advice!

Katie Pitt's father owned the 6-acre field at Shear Hill, which had been filled with tanks for two or three months before D-Day. All down the side of the road to Portsmouth tanks were parked for weeks; Katie remembers the enormous roar on D-Day itself as hundreds of planes flew past overhead and the tanks moved off from beside their house down to Portsmouth. She got a call to report to the Queen Alexandra Hospital where two hundred surgeons and nurses had been drafted in to work twenty-four hours a day. Mary Ray remembers that she was staying with a friend in Woodbury Avenue when they heard the throbbing drone of Dakotas overhead at about 4 a.m.; they looked up to see the grey shapes of the planes towing gliders and heading towards the south (the planes had been painted with zebra stripes on each wing and around their fuselage so that Allied troops on the ground would recognise them as friendly aircraft); by midday people knew that the Normandy landings had at last happened. Later that day Emanuel School was playing cricket at Charterhouse – the epitome of an English summer scene! – as the planes and gliders passed by overhead on their way to the greatest military invasion ever seen; the incongruity of the situation did not escape the young sportsmen!

ENTERTAINMENTS

One effect of the ban on movement within the Prohibited Areas was to cause the postponement of the Petersfield Musical Festival until the autumn. At least that was the provision made by the organisers, but in fact the Festival did not take place in 1944 at all, the only year since its inception in 1901 (apart from during the First World War) that this had happened. Despite Sir Adrian Boult's willingness to conduct – he had been quoted as saying: 'for me, two choirs with one man each would make a festival' – it had to be abandoned.

Over the Easter period Petersfield's need for musical and dramatic entertainment was, as usual, amply catered for. The staff of Emanuel School put on Turgenev's *A Month in the Country*, while Bedales orchestra and choir performed Handel's *Messiah*, and at the Savoy cinema Laurel and Hardy's *A-Hunting We Will Go* provided some light entertainment.

However, the town was remarkably quiet that Easter, owing to the enforced ban on movement in the area. There were not a lot of visitors and those who did come were subject to quite a detailed inspection of identity cards and questioning by the police, assisted by the Home Guard.

NEW OPTIMISM

It was evident that a certain degree of optimism began to be felt at this time as it became clear that the end of the war was in sight. In the *Squeaker* there were signs of deliberations about the postwar period. The Midland Bank inserted an advert headed 'Business enterprise after the war', and the first in a series of articles about postwar housing in Petersfield was published. In addition to these considerations there was a prolonged discussion about the proposed new Education Bill which would be published by the government later in 1944.

On the war front a 'Salute the Soldier' campaign started in the spring which soon reached its target. At its annual general meeting the Rural District Council's Salvage Officer, Mr P.P. Chamings, reported on a house (now Steep House Nursing Home) he had had occasion to visit which was being used as a hostel for Free French Navy personnel in the district. In particular, he congratulated the establishment on its excellent attention paid to public health, which reflected well on the lady in charge, Madame Maze, described by Jean Pritchard as 'a very distinguished and formidable woman'. There was no doubt that it was a real home-from-home for the French visitors who passed through its doors.

Arising out of a Town Planning Committee report at a meeting of the Urban District Council in the summer, it was announced that the Misses Townsend and Mrs Gibson had written to offer a meadow of nearly 3 acres to the town. This meadow, abutting on Swan Street and Frenchman's Road and adjoining Highfield House and garden, was being offered as a gift to the town in perpetuity. The lady benefactors wished the town to benefit from the use of the land as a public open space for all time, and the name chosen for the plot was to be High Meadow.

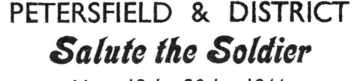

PETERSFIELD & DISTRICT
Salute the Soldier
May 13th—20th, 1944

THE TARGET: £230,000
(equip and maintain a base hospital for one year)

The decisive period of the war approaches. In the West the Allies are crouched for the spring, muscles braced, nerves taut. A heavy task faces the soldier. What can we do to help him? Compared to his sacrifice, Little. But in effect Much. We can SAVE and lend to provide the armour, without which all his sacrifice will be in vain. Thus do we

SALUTE THE SOLDIER

Advert in the Hants and Sussex News, *Salute the Soldier Campaign, 1944. (Hampshire Museums Service)*

High Meadow, donated to the town by the Townsend family in 1944. (Author's Collection)

The WVS (Women's Voluntary Service) report to the UDC revealed the extent of its numerous beneficial activities during the war: it ran an emergency clothing store with premises in The Square, a children's clothing exchange and an emergency nursery for householders in times of illness; it distributed Wellington boots to all schools and collected books for salvage; it organised lectures on how to 'make-do-and-mend'; it had over forty cars available and a pool of volunteer drivers to deliver produce and dinners to hospitals and cocoa and jam to children's hostels; it supplied 'comforts' (clothing and cigarettes) for the Merchant Navy and collected vegetables for 'the little ships' at the time of Dunkirk; it supplied mobile canteens for the Civil Defence and the Home Guard; and it opened a factory for making camouflage nets.

The Home from Home canteen in College Street served its millionth meal in September 1944 when it celebrated the third anniversary of its existence. Its operational peak had been reached in the week immediately before D-Day (6 June), when over 15,000 meals were served as hundreds of troops passed through the town on their way to Portsmouth. September 1944 was also the fifth anniversary of the outbreak of war and the fourth anniversary of the Battle of Britain. Fittingly, a service of thanksgiving and remembrance was held in St Peter's church.

As further signs of normality gradually returned to Petersfield, the autumn brought the Taro Fair, held 'under brighter, and in view of the much more hopeful war situation, happier conditions than since 1938'. The *Squeaker* reported that there seemed to be 'a light-heartedness about the public indulgence in the interest and amusement provided which indicated the popularity of this annual festival, still evidently a red-letter day for country folk'. Commercial life was picking up too and the *Squeaker* started to carry more advertisements in its pages: the Petersfield and District Laundry announced that it could now offer a collection and delivery service on a weekly basis, and George Bailey, the nurseryman and seedsman in Chapel Street, was offering 'a fine selection of first-class bulbs' for planting. Furthermore, it was no longer necessary to retain the services of any members of the Fire Guard staff and notice had been given to the Fire Guard Officer (Mr Stafford) and shorthand-typist (Miss Davis) that they would no longer be required after 15 November. Following authorisation received from the Ministry for Home Security, main street lighting in Petersfield was restored in October and steps were being taken to complete the lighting of the town as quickly as possible. Despite these measures, there was no certainty that air raids would cease in the area; however, road blocks were removed in November.

IN THE SCHOOLS

At the end of the school year in 1944 Emanuel expressed its debt to Petersfield, West Mark Camp School showed its appreciation in its Sports Day speeches, and the School Harvest Camps earned further praise for their organisers.

Mr Broom once again thanked the foster parents of the Emanuel boys, laying the credit with them for the fact that the school had maintained one of the highest numbers of boys in evacuation of all London schools. They were equally indebted to Mr Wilkins, the Chief Billeting Officer, whose office had had a particularly harmonious relationship with the school. The school was looking forward to the time when they could return to London, but it seemed unlikely that this would happen by the start of the new school year in September. On behalf of the school, Mr Broom surrendered the allotments which the Council had allowed them to use at Sheet, so that they could become available to the town's residents. Apart from the valuable personal training the boys had had in the war effort, he thought they had made a useful addition to the food supplies obtainable in the town.

Mr Hawkins, speaking at West Mark Camp School's annual Sports Day, reminded the parents present that, although their type of school was a product of the war, it had afforded everyone the chance to see the benefit of boarding education and a communal life. It was clearly to the liking of the children too: of those who had left in 1944, the average length of time they had stayed in Petersfield was seventeen months, a considerable improvement on previous years. There were still eleven children left who had come as the 'pioneers' in 1940. The qualities of self-reliance, consideration for others and the joy of working for a community all left their mark, as did the strict routine of the school's timetable. Sir Edward Howarth, Managing Director of the National Camps Corporation, congratulated West Mark on being one of the finest of the thirty camp schools throughout England. Such schools, he said, gave children a feeling for the country, some sense of what it meant, and, above all, provided the simple pleasures of the country which were of tremendous value in their future lives.

But camp schools were not the only opportunity for children to appreciate the values of country life: about thirty Schoolboy Harvest Camps were operating in Hampshire at this time. Emanuel School had also taken advantage of this scheme, which had begun in order to provide useful work for the boys who could not return to London during the Battle of Britain in the first summer of the war. Under the charge of Mr H.B. Mearns, the Emanuel Harvesting Camp took place at Heath Road East, and during the first week, forty-six boys worked for eight or nine hours a day. For recreation at the end of the day there was a large marquee erected for music concerts, with electric light, and a resident cook, who won the hearts of all the boys.

At the Petersfield County High School for Girls Speech Day, it was reported that more girls than previously had stayed on after School Certificate (taken at the age of sixteen) and the school roll stood at 180 in total. Since the building had been designed for only 100 pupils, it was still necessary for many classes to be held elsewhere in the town, such as the Girl Guides' hut or the Congregational Schoolroom, even, in the case of music, in teachers' private houses.

At an annual display by Battersea Central School the Headmistress, Miss Cocksedge, voiced the hope that the school would be returning to London by the following Easter and she also thanked the Petersfield hosts for their kindness in providing homes for the girls.

THE DIMINISHING WAR SITUATION

The Normandy landings had taken place six months previously and the mood was for talk of eventual victory and new peacetime conditions. The 'stand down' of the Home Guard in Petersfield and district took place shortly before Christmas. The 15th Battalion of the Hampshire Home Guard assembled at the railway station and marched through the town, General Sir Alexander Wardrop taking the salute in The Square, and on to the Town Hall car park, where valedictory speeches were made.

Although not yet demobilised, another volunteer force (and one which was said to consider itself the elite of the voluntary services), the Royal Observer Corps, was also near to the end of its useful existence. Founded in 1935, its system of day and night watches had continued throughout the war and, as an adjunct of the RAF, it had played a particularly important role during the Battle of Britain. Altogether there were about 35,000 men and women in this arm of Civil Defence nationally. The 1,500 posts which they had manned were chiefly created to look out for

German planes, but also guided 'distressed' Allied aircraft home, reported crashes into the sea and tracked flying bombs. Mary Ray's father, Guy Pearson, had joined the Observer Corps in 1939 and the local group had its official post at Froxfield, but met regularly at the Welcome Inn in Station Road (now Meon Close). In 1944 the Chief Observer, Alan Hinxman (the cattle auctioneer and boss of Hall, Pain and Foster), read a notice calling for volunteers for a Seaborne Observer Force to serve with the Normandy Invasion Fleet in Merchant Ships. Eight local men volunteered.

In December 1944 the number and consequences of air raids in the Petersfield urban and rural districts since the beginning of the war until February 1944 were published as follows:

	Urban	Rural
Casualties: killed	7	7
seriously injured	11	2
slightly injured	5	3
Machine-gun attacks	2	5
High Explosive bombs	23	421
Mines	0	16
Anti-personnel attacks	0	1
Oil bombs	2	12
Phosphorus	0	2
Other incendiary attacks	1	22
Properties: destroyed	0	0
damaged and irreparable	1	3
badly damaged	1	6
slightly damaged	27	519

In a report to the Rural District Council Sir Hugh Cocke said that arrangements were now being made for evacuees to return to Portsmouth, Gosport and Southampton. There were now 1,320 evacuees in Petersfield, representing 450 family units (of which 350 were from Portsmouth). Sir Hugh thought that about 40 per cent of these had accommodation to which they could return. Petersfield would be faced with about 200–300 families without accommodation to return to. Unaccompanied children, of which there were about 200, were in this category, except for the Portsmouth High School girls who were still resident at Adhurst St Mary.

D-Day was not followed by a sudden victory, however; instead came the V1 bombs. As Norman Longmate explains:

The first flying bombs (V1s) clattered across the Channel in June 1944. Of all the bombs that descended upon the British Isles between 1939 and 1945, none is remembered with more bitter loathing. This first unmanned aircraft, with its harsh-sounding engine, scuttling remorselessly across the sky like some science-fiction monster, seemed even more sinister than the bombers which preceded it.

Herbert Morrison felt it necessary to warn the public that 'when the engine of the pilotless aircraft stops and the light at the end of the machine is seen to go out, it may mean that an explosion will soon follow, perhaps in five to fifteen seconds'. Technically identified as 'flying bombs', the V1s soon became known as 'buzz bombs' or 'doodlebugs'. David Martin remembers coming home from Churcher's one Friday afternoon and hearing the engine of a doodlebug stopping over Petersfield; people looked upwards in great fear, but the machine continued its flight path to Froxfield, where it crashed without causing any loss of life.

CHRISTMAS 1944

Christmas was marked for fifty Petersfield children of the Junior Council School in St Peter's Road by the invitation from a very special Santa Claus to meet him at his Canadian camp nearby. Two lorries and a car transported the children and some of the teachers there; they were met with a fine welcome, 'movies', games, treasure-hunts, ice creams, tea with Christmas cake, and the gift of a Christmas stocking and an apple for each of them.

The sixth Christmas of the war could not be celebrated with outright merry-making, yet the Home from Home canteen determined that the servicemen and women should have a properly festive time. On 17 December 'The Merrymakers Concert Party' set the seasonal scene, culminating in a grand plum pudding stirring ceremony; on 23 December 800 people went to the Town Hall for a Christmas dance, with music by the 'Cossack' Dance Band; on Christmas Eve there was a variety entertainment given by Mrs Money-Chappelle's guest artistes; on Christmas Day itself, 300 guests enjoyed a party at the canteen; on Boxing Day a dinner was held, followed by a dance; the day after that another grand ball took place at the Town Hall with music by the Army School of Hygiene Dance Band; and finally, on New Year's Eve, the festivities were brought to a close with the singing of 'Auld Lang Syne' and a blessing and wish from the Chaplain, Canon Money, for a happy and victorious New Year.

CHAPTER SEVEN

1945

Slow Recovery & Changing Times

GROUP FOR THE PRESERVATION & IMPROVEMENT OF PETERSFIELD

In September 1944 two exhibitions were held in Petersfield, one of photographs and the other of pictures and sketches depicting charming views of the older parts of the town. Three months later the shop window of 2 High Street (John Dowler's, now New Look) was used to display a combined exhibition by the Photographic and the Arts and Crafts Societies, drawing public attention to buildings which had been demolished, such as the much regretted Castle House, pulled down in 1911, and those of architectural importance which remained. A tremendous amount of interest was aroused in many quarters: schools were contacted and their pupils flocked to see the exhibition, about 1,500 people were sent letters asking for their support and opinions, and a lantern slide show of the exhibits was created to stimulate further interest.

Concurrently, it was under the title 'Group for the Preservation and Improvement of Petersfield' that a letter to the *Squeaker* caught the notice of the general public. Written by Edward Barnsley and Mary Ward, Chairman and Hon. Secretary respectively of the newly formed group, it outlined their objectives thus:

1. To develop and increase public interest in the beauty of Petersfield and its neighbourhood and in the future planning within the area.
2. To focus this general interest and direct it into channels of practical work, in which members of the community may take part and contribute to postwar planning.
3. To build up a strong body of public opinion supporting the Planning Authorities in their difficult task of ensuring that building and development is organised to achieve the maximum possible degree of harmony.

This group, inaugurated by the Petersfield Photographic and Arts and Crafts Societies, was clearly stepping in at a crucial moment in the town's history. Fearful that the natural beauty of the town and its environs might be irretrievably damaged or at least compromised by the planning authorities in the postwar era, its members saw it as their duty to promote public awareness of such issues as the architectural heritage and aesthetic beauty of the town.

Repercussions from this development were rapidly felt over the next two months with the publication of a series of four articles by M. Roland-Pullen entitled 'Petersfield: Past, Present and Future'. Claiming impartiality by being neither a native nor a resident of the town, 'M.R.P.', as he signed himself to begin with, clearly had the future interests of Petersfield at heart and knew the town extremely well.

During the course of the early part of 1945, therefore, these expressions of concern for the future character of the town were to help create an open debate and formulate opinion on postwar Petersfield. What is perhaps more interesting was the author's preoccupation with the almost imperceptible nature of change itself, but also to the predictable anxiety over the imminent social and commercial upheavals which were to come about on a national scale in the immediate postwar years.

Mr Roland-Pullen, denying that he was being in any way over-sentimental in calling Petersfield 'a piece of old England' or suggesting that one should cling unconditionally to the picturesque, nevertheless wanted to guard against eyesores (or 'Clanfields' as he typified them – no doubt recalling the purely makeshift constructions which had been put up there in the war). He reiterated the fundamental considerations of the new 'Preservation and Improvement of Petersfield' group in calling for the safe keeping of the beautiful architecture in the town, citing the High Street as an example where styles from the seventeenth to the twentieth century stood harmoniously together. He advocated the use only of the least valuable agricultural land for any further extension of the town into the countryside, the vigorous rejection of any building development close to the Heath, and the careful siting of light industries in order that they should not endanger the surrounding areas such as Bell Hill and Steep. He also emphasised the importance of a 'warm' atmosphere to buildings which 'super-modern' architecture did not afford, while multiple shops, with their standardised shop-fronts, were anathema to him.

Several of Roland-Pullen's arguments were clearly subjective, however, and, as with the views of all amateur critics, there was a good deal of the self-evident and superficial in his comments. Although he wanted care to be taken over the development of the eastern side of The Square (compared to the 'successful' removal and replacement of Castle House effected on the western side), he seemed unconcerned about replacing the properties in Church Path and Sheep Street, since they 'scarcely afford adequate living accommodation'.

Inevitably, time has caught up with 'M.R.P.' and his observations on the mis-siting of the Town Hall (he feels it could have been built on the site of the old Corn Exchange), the 'jerry-building' era which produced the Savoy cinema (which lacks 'finish'), and the 'anachronisms' of Sheep Street, Dog Alley and North Road now appear ill-judged and have themselves become anachronistic.

In his last article 'M.R.P.' perhaps partially redeemed himself in reminding readers that the central core of Petersfield should remain The Square, that building materials should relate to their surroundings (modern red brick and tiles may more easily blend with earlier styles than white stone or plaster), and that the use of chromium (rather than wood) for Mr Bailey's new shop-front at 1 Chapel Street would not have sat well with Flora Twort's flint and half-timbered bookshop next door at 1 The Square. He concluded his articles by listing the amenities which he felt were lacking in the town: inadequate recreational facilities for children and a central educational facility in Love Lane (agreeing here with Mrs Lubbock and Harry Roberts), while deploring the highway congestion caused by the two major through roads in the town.

The concerns of individuals and groups regarding the future development of the town became formalised with the announcement that the Society for the Preservation and Improvement of Petersfield, which had been mooted in the press some nine months earlier and which had garnered considerable support since (with a membership after six months' existence of over 800), was to be reconstituted under the name of The Petersfield Society. Its first meeting took place on 21 July 1945.

VE DAY

The sudden death on 12 April of the American President, Franklin Delano Roosevelt, led to the Stars and Stripes being flown at half-mast on the premises of a leading Petersfield business establishment; at St Peter's church the congregation stood in silence while the 'Star Spangled Banner' was played on the organ.

In the town, preparations for celebrating the triumph of the Allies were beginning even before Mr Churchill's official announcement of the Victory in Europe on Tuesday 8 May. Flags had already been hung out on the Monday, and by the Tuesday morning shops, streets and houses were festooned with bunting, the flags of the Allies and other decorations. On that Tuesday, the first day of national celebration, food shops were open until lunchtime, then closed as everyone thronged into the town to celebrate along with a good number of Service personnel. After a school assembly a great mass of boys marched out from Churcher's College arm in arm, singing all the way up the flag-bedecked High Street, round the town and back to The Square, where the statue of William of Orange was draped with school ties and scarves. Churchill's message was re-broadcast from various places and, later, a great crowd flocked to thanksgiving services.

On their own initiative that evening the Emanuel School jazz band, the Windsor Rhythm Kings, started the celebrations. They installed themselves on top of the air-raid shelter in front of St Peter's, rigged up a string of coloured electric lights between there and the statue of King William III (sporting 'unconventional headgear!'), and soon many people had gathered round to listen and there was dancing until well into the night. Mary and David Vincent remember enjoying jitterbugging (the latest US dance craze) to the music! The boys took advantage of the atmosphere of goodwill and started a collection for the Emanuel School Fund, to raise an endowment for a bed at Petersfield Hospital to commemorate their association with the town. The sum of £500 was raised, and this was donated to the hospital before their departure from Petersfield.

As had previously been promised in the *Squeaker*, a free dance and community singing had taken place at the Town Hall on Tuesday evening. The following Sunday a VE Day Service of Thanksgiving was held by Petersfield churches at the Town Hall and attended by the numerous organisations which had played their part in the war effort: the ARP, the Police, the Fire Service, the Boy Scouts and Girl Guides, the Red Cross, the Junior Training Corps, the Women's Land Army and the Civil Defence Reserve among others. Norma Collins clearly remembers the mass of choirs which sang that day in celebration.

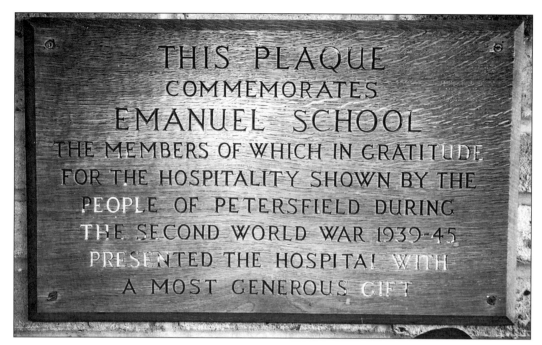

A plaque commemorating Emanuel School's gift to Petersfield hospital in 1945. (Author's Collection)

The victory celebrations in Petersfield took many forms: four dances were held within a week in May, two children's parties were organised for younger and older children and there were street parties of all kinds throughout the town. One of these was held in Madeline Road, where an afternoon of games was organised in the road, followed by a tea for seventy children and adults served on tables adorned with flags and other trimmings. A similar event was held for the residents of Highfield and Tilmore Roads, with a procession headed by the 1st Petersfield Boys' Brigade Bugle Band, leading about eighty children to a sports afternoon at the Girls' High School playing field. Peggy Carpenter remembers a penny-a-week collection for the celebrations and trestle tables suddenly appearing in the middle of roads for impromptu street parties. An open-air tea party was held in front of Hadlow Terrace in the Causeway, and the children of North Stroud Lane had their tea in the Lane, followed by races, games and community singing.

During two days of celebrations at the Home from Home canteen on 8 and 9 May, over 2,500 free meals were served to members of all the Services. A big crowd gathered there at 3 p.m. on 8 May to listen to Winston Churchill's victory broadcast and in the evening there was dancing in the hall. Vic Walker went to another dance at the Welcome Inn; all over Petersfield there were all-night celebrations.

As a climax to the victory rejoicings in Petersfield a gigantic tea party, followed by entertainment for children between the ages of five and fourteen was given by the Urban District Council at the Town Hall. Nearly 700 children assembled and were welcomed by the Chairman, George Bailey. In the beflagged and bedecked hall, there was an excellent tea provided by the staff of the British Restaurant, followed by singing, a conjuror and a farewell bar of chocolate for every child, given by an anonymous donor. Steve Pibworth was backstage at the time, but remembers the excellent playing of the band.

The Headmistress of the Junior Council School, Eulalie Matson, wrote to the *Squeaker* to thank the Council for providing what one small lad in her school had called 'the happiest day of my life'.

Katie Pitt describes the end of the war as 'like coming out of an anaesthetic'. In fact for everyone the moment was something of an anti-climax: rapid adjustments had to be made to individuals' lives, the return of men from the Services was still awaited, commercial life would be slow to pick up again, Petersfield was about to lose the vast numbers of youngsters who had spent their war years in the town, and families had to reconstitute themselves for the new – and unpredictable – peace. Regrettably, the well-known and established grocery and provision merchant's business of Mr J.P. Cordery in College Street (now Antrobus House) ceased trading a month later, after eighty years as a family firm in the town. Was this a sign of the times to come in Petersfield?

ELECTIONEERING

No sooner had the victory celebrations died down than electioneering began in earnest in June 1945. The 67-year-old General Sir George Jeffreys (Conservative and National Party), who had been returned unopposed for the constituency of East Hampshire in 1941 in succession to Sir Reginald Dorman-Smith, found himself opposed this time by two men in their thirties: Flight Lieutenant Basil Goldstone (Liberal) and the Commonwealth Party candidate Tom Sargant, who had the support of the Labour Party in the absence of Lieutenant Colonel Muir Hunter who was still serving in India. However, it was reported by all three candidates during the hustings that there appeared to be little excitement for this election on the part of the electors. After counting had taken place later in the month the result showed a substantial majority for General Sir George Jeffreys, with over 20,000 votes against about 8,000 for Flight Lieutenant Goldstone and 6,000 for Mr Sargant.

DEREQUISITIONING & DEMOBILISATION

Wartime organisations gradually wound down their activities: the ARP and the Civil Defence structures ceased and thanks to those responsible were expressed at the Urban District Council meeting in June 1945. The derequisitioning of premises had by now begun and was proceeding rapidly.

At a meeting of the Urban District Council the previous February, arrangements had already been discussed for the reception of the men and women returning from war service and 'to recognise in some beneficial fashion what they have contributed to its successful prosecution'. At a public meeting in the Town Hall suggestions for marking this event included the building of a reference library with attached reading room and games room, the construction of a swimming pool, a community centre, a Red Cross centre and the provision of gardens and rest places. This report naturally resulted in a debate in the *Squeaker* in which one correspondent even suggested the levelling of the tumuli on the Heath as a site for the swimming pool!

The idea of an open-air swimming pool clearly caught the public imagination and, with the receipts from the 'Welcome Home Fund' set up in the town later in 1945, the decision was taken to build one. The pool was eventually maintained by the UDC and it became Council property.

THE EVACUEES RETURN HOME

In common with the other Heads of the evacuated schools in Petersfield, the Headmistress of the Battersea Central School, Miss K. Cocksedge, reported that the school would be departing at the end of the school year in July. Her thanks to the town and the host families were expressed in a letter to the *Squeaker*:

> For nearly six years, we have had the privilege of living in Petersfield and the surrounding districts and have met with extreme kindness and consideration from almost everyone. We shall return to London with very mixed feelings, for all of us have learnt to love Petersfield and I know that the memories of our time here will live in our hearts through the years to come.

At the school's Sports Day that summer more tributes were paid, this time to their Tilmore playing field, which was described as 'the gem set among the hills', of which the returning Londoners would treasure happy memories.

A letter written to the *Daily Express* newspaper by Mr A.J. Wilkins, Petersfield's Chief Billeting Officer, mentioning the rough figure of a thousand unaccompanied children billeted in the town during the war (of which a few hundred still remained), drew the following response from a correspondent to the *Squeaker*: 'Had other areas put into the Evacuation Scheme the hard work and kindliness lavished on it by Petersfield officials and townsfolk, there would have been no breakdowns, and a great many class and geographical rivalries would have been lessened throughout the country.'

As the two main groups of evacuee schoolchildren finished their academic year in Petersfield, thanks were given for the hospitality which had been extended to them in the town: in a lengthy letter to many different parties the Emanuel School Headmaster, Second Master, Chairman and Secretary of the Common Room and the Captain of the school warmly thanked individuals in Petersfield who had ensured the maintenance of the life of Emanuel School during the six years of the war, in particular the self-sacrifice and unremitting care of the foster-parents. Throughout the war Emanuel School had presented an annual concert for their host families in appreciation of the help they had received. The farewell wish was expressed thus:

May Petersfield, amid all the coming changes and developments, remain a haven of beauty and peace, as it will assuredly retain a charm for the Londoners who have come to know and love it.

Two of the evacuees' hostesses wrote a touching letter to the *Squeaker* in reply:

The time is drawing very near when we are to lose the majority of our wartime visitors. They have said some very kind and charming things about Petersfield and I am sure we are voicing the feelings of others besides ourselves when we say how very much they will be missed. They have brought us many good things – young life into our rather middle-aged community, music, drama, intellectual stimulus and a general broadening of outlook. In addition, they have thrown themselves into the life of the town, especially in the way of clerical help, ARP, Home Guard, and when our public institution was blitzed, and in many other ways. In spite of any extra troubles their stay here may have entailed, Petersfield will be the poorer for their departure.

Emanuel School's departure from Petersfield was commemorated by a farewell gathering in the Town Hall, which consisted of an entertainment of songs, solo instrumental playing, burlesque and impersonations by the staff and boys, followed by the donation of a cheque for 25 guineas to Churcher's College to endow a prize. The actual departure from the station was the occasion for a significant demonstration of the strong ties which had been formed between the school and the town, as hundreds of hostesses and other friends assembled to bid their farewells. Churcher's College JTC and band paraded at the station in their honour. Peter Lyne was the house prefect designated to be in charge of hiring the lorries to transport the Emanuel School materials (stocked initially at the back of the Sun Inn in what was irreverently called 'The Dump') back to London. He travelled up and down on each of the eight journeys it took to complete this task. In fact, as the numbers of pupils at Emanuel School evacuated to Petersfield reduced as the end of the war came into sight, there were only 229 boys returning in 1945, half the number who had originally come in 1939. Emanuel School had felt obliged to re-open their London premises from September 1943 to the minority of younger boys (fewer than 100 under fourteens) who had chosen to stay in Wandsworth and follow the emergency tutorial classes organised by the London County Council. Subsequently, Major Charles Hill and a few other members of staff were despatched from Petersfield to take charge of this mini-school.

The Battersea Central School left Petersfield on 13 July, 'with a real sense of regret at leaving behind so many kind friends, who will be equally sorry to lose them'. Before leaving Petersfield the school sent a cheque for £25 to the Methodist church in acknowledgement of the great kindness they had experienced in the welcome and accommodation provided in the Methodist schoolroom, with the request that something might be purchased as a memento of the pleasant and helpful association of the church and school.

Of course, it was not just the schoolchildren who were returning home. In October a letter received from Madame Maze of Steep House was read out at Petersfield Petty Sessions by the Clerk, Mr A.J.C. Mackarness. It concerned the hospitality received by the Free French sailors in Petersfield and read as follows:

The Steep House is closing down on the 29th September next, and it has been a great help and great comfort for our sailors to spend quiet and happy days in this delightful place when they were deprived, through German occupation, of going to their homes. We shall never be grateful enough to England for her kind hospitality, and in particular to the Petersfield people for their kindness and all they did for us. We shall never forget, and when things will be easier, we hope to have you all among us in France. Many thanks.

COMMEMORATIVE EVENTS

HMS *Primula*, Petersfield's adopted ship, was decommissioned in July. She had been engaged on escort work for most of the war, running supplies to Tobruk and all over the Mediterranean. Lieutenant Commander E. Wilding and ten of his crew visited the town in August. They brought the ship's ensign which was presented to St Peter's church as a reminder of the relationship between ship and town during the war; Lieutenant Commander Wilding also presented a silver cup to be called the Primula Cup for competition among the schools of Petersfield. The ship's wooden crest, with an embossed primula at its centre, was presented to the town

The wooden crest of HMS Primula. (Petersfield Museum)

and district councils who were to hold it in alternate years. Finally, a surplus of £445 from the Primula Fund, which had been raised by the town, was donated to Petersfield Hospital to dedicate a bed in the name of 'HM Corvette *Primula*'.

VJ (Victory over Japan) Day, officially Tuesday 15 August, was a much more low-key affair than VE Day had been. Two days of national holidays were announced for the Wednesday and Thursday, and on the Wednesday business was suspended, except for a few hours in the morning when food shops stayed open. The cattle market in The Square took place as usual. People roamed the streets and gathered in The Square, where there was dancing to music, first from a radiogram, then from live bands in the evening. A service of thanksgiving took place in St Peter's church.

Two stained-glass windows commemorating the connection of Canadian troops with the parish were unveiled at Bramshott church in 1945.

Thanksgiving Week in October was an opportunity to persuade people that savings were still important to rebuild the country in the National Reconstruction programme, especially, in the Petersfield area, to raise funds for new homes and new schools.

At Churcher's College Speech Day in November the fate of Old Churcherians in the war was, of course, uppermost in people's minds. Vic Walker has since catalogued the details of the fifty-three Old Churcherians (staff and boys) who lost their lives in the war. Masters and pupils received fifty-one awards, including four DSOs (Distinguished Service Order), three DSCs (Distinguished Service Cross), eleven MCs (Military Cross) and ten DFCs (Distinguished Flying Cross).

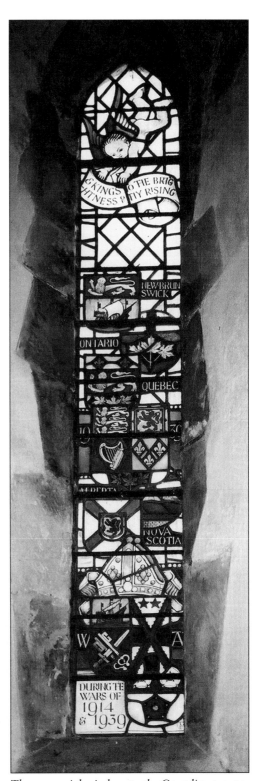

The memorial window to the Canadian troops in Bramshott church. (Author's Collection)

Sat. October 13th—20th, 1945

Why we must still SAVE

The Prime Minister, speaking at the opening of London's Week on Sept. 15th said : " Let no one doubt that his individual savings are being put to good use in the National Reconstruction programme—the repair of war damage, the building of new houses, new schools and public services : the revival of trade, particularly the export trade.　For these, savings are essential."

Again : " If we relax all controls and try to spend our money while there is a shortage of goods, prices will rise . . . and your shillings will buy less."

Here in Petersfield & District your money will go especially to build new homes, better school premises. By lending all you can you will be paying some part of the debt to the men who fought and who will soon be returning.　That is the best welcome you can give them.

Issued by the Petersfield & District National Savings Committee.

Advert in the Hants and Sussex News, *Thanksgiving Week, 1945. (Hampshire Museums Service)*

THE TRIBUTE TO THE HOME FROM HOME CANTEEN

Tributes to the Home from Home canteen were paid at what was described as 'its last birthday anniversary' in September. In fact, the 'Home from Home' was asked to remain open for a further year, owing to urgent requests received from welfare branches of the Army and Navy. Kathleen Money-Chappelle regretfully asked her Management Committee to accept her resignation as Honorary Organiser. However, the committee begged her to continue her work as organiser, but with a salary, and she agreed to remain 'a while longer'. Mrs Money-Chappelle said that she had mixed feelings about the closure: joy at the end of the war, tinged with regret that their days of working together were over. In thanking her for her great energy, enterprise and devoted work, Lord Horder presented Mrs Money-Chappelle with a wristwatch of white gold set with diamonds and remarked that she 'could not have done many things in her life, nor would she live long enough to do many more things quite as good as [the canteen]'.

EDUCATIONAL CHANGES

With the departure of the many hundreds of evacuated schoolchildren who had been educated in Petersfield during the war, the future educational needs of the town came under discussion. At local and county level it was the location of new schools which continued to exercise political minds. Of all the sites proposed for a future 'modern school', the education authorities seemed particularly wedded to the Causeway site where, according to the Hampshire County Council Education Officer, the require-ment was for a 'multilateral school', embodying the different types of education for about 480–500 girls, with a further similar school near to Churcher's College to cater for boys. At the same time a site for a junior school was also identified in Love Lane.

With the coming of the new 1944 Education Act the Senior Council School in St Peter's Road changed its name at the end of the war to the Petersfield Secondary Modern School (or 'PSM') and even introduced caps and badges, although few families could afford these immediately. Simultaneously, the debate began about whether a single-sex or mixed school was preferable for the town, yet it would be over a decade before the new purpose-built building beside the Causeway was completed (in 1958) to satisfy the increasing demand for secondary school places for both boys and girls in Petersfield; school rolls had increased dramatically with the raising of the school leaving age to fifteen in 1947.

Churcher's College's position was in some doubt in September 1945, as its application for Direct Grant status had been turned down by the Minister of Education (despite having the approval of the Hampshire Education Committee), possibly owing to its weak financial position. However, the Headmaster's optimism regarding the school's future as a day and boarding school, accepting boys from outside the immediate area of Petersfield, seemed to assure parents that the school would continue in its current form for a long time to come. In fact, it became fully independent in 1979.

One piece of news which caused some regret, though not surprise, was the announcement of the impending retirement of Mr Hoggarth, the Headmaster, who had decided to leave the school at Easter 1946 after eighteen years in his post (although he had in fact been on the staff since 1911). When he had come to the school there had been 140 pupils; when he left there were 351. His successor was to be Mr G.T. Schofield. With the departure of the bachelor Mr Hoggarth and the imminent arrival of Mr Schofield, who had a family, it was necessary to find a new boarding house for the younger preparatory boys, who had previously lived and studied in the house donated to Churcher's by Mr Heath Harrison for the use of the Headmaster. This necessity for a move was turned into a virtue by Jack Le Grice, who had been in charge of the old preparatory school and who now bought the large property opposite the school known as Broadlands and transformed it into a new prep school, with himself as Headmaster.

Concurrently, there were to be other changes in the educational field in Petersfield: at the Girls' High School Speech Day it was announced that Miss Emma Lowde, who had been its Headmistress since the school opened in 1918, was to leave, while at Bedales, Freddie Meier's headship was coming to an end and he was to be replaced by Hector Jacks in March 1946. Within a couple of years of the war ending Miss Williams' tenure as Headmistress at Winton House was also at an end and the school closed with her departure.

SLOW RECOVERY

On Armistice Day, 11 November, which, being a Sunday, coincided with Remembrance Day that year, three boys living at Reservoir Cottages had a miraculous escape when interfering with a mortar bomb that they had picked up on the military ranges on Butser Hill and brought home. They were in a shed as the bomb exploded; it blew one of the boys out of the open door, the shed windows were blown out and the three boys received injuries to their faces. 'This should be a warning to young people' was the curt response from the *Squeaker*.

By the end of the year life was getting back to normal again in Petersfield and residual signs of wartime were being removed one by one: Nissen huts on the Heath were to be removed shortly, along with the demolition of ARP shelters in the town; the British Legion canteen in St Peter's hall, which had opened in January 1940 and been patronised by thousands of servicemen and women, was finally closed after operating for six years, mainly at the weekends. However, the government stated that they hoped people would keep their respirators (gas masks) 'in case they were required again'.

Rationing took many years to disappear from people's daily lives after the war: clothes rationing continued until 1949, petrol rationing until 1950 and food rationing did not finally come to an end until 1954. Food parcels from Australia, New Zealand and America were still being received by Petersfield schoolchildren in 1946 and 1947. In view of its reduced role in the town, especially since the departure of the evacuees, the Petersfield Food Office moved from Station Road to three Nissen huts behind the Town Hall in 1949. Some children discovered bananas for the first time after the war, and weren't sure at first if they should peel them or not!

In a fascinating article published on 8 August 1945 and entitled 'Petersfield Revisited', the *Squeaker* reported the comments made by a correspondent (identified only as A.B.C.) comparing the town with his memory of it when he left it as a young boy in 1902. Some of the outlying parts of the town had, naturally, been transformed by new construction with varying effect: the Causeway, for example, was now much more populated, but Rushes Farm at the bottom of Bell Hill had gone, leaving a pleasanter walk to the top. Petersfield's streets, he continued, were

Graeme Triggs in his father's shop, which remained unchanged from the 1930s until the 1990s. (*Author's Collection*)

cleaner and tidier now, but he preferred the old Castle House (demolished in 1913) to the new post office and Midland Bank buildings (constructed in 1922). On Lavant Street, 'I have yet to console myself that the breaking out of the villa-type houses into shops is not a detriment to that street, but business demands space.' Perhaps the first fifty years of the twentieth-century history of the town were destined to reflect the next fifty: some of the features of that growth – the disappearance of some of the 'urban' farms, the orderly aspect of new buildings, the slow commercialisation of Lavant Street – also characterised the changes which beset Petersfield in the next half-century.

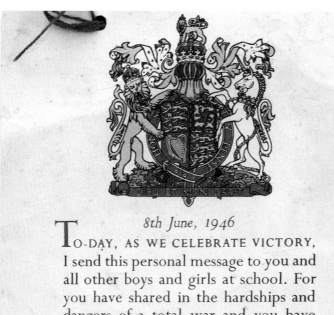

8th June, 1946

TO-DAY, AS WE CELEBRATE VICTORY, I send this personal message to you and all other boys and girls at school. For you have shared in the hardships and dangers of a total war and you have shared no less in the triumph of the Allied Nations.

I know you will always feel proud to belong to a country which was capable of such supreme effort; proud, too, of parents and elder brothers and sisters who by their courage, endurance and enterprise brought victory. May these qualities be yours as you grow up and join in the common effort to establish among the nations of the world unity and peace.

George R.I.

King George VI's message to schoolchildren a year after the war. (Chris Lloyd Collection)

Conclusion:
Postwar Petersfield

Politically, the postwar situation under the new Attlee government changed fast, although it was short-lived (Churchill's first administration for the Conservatives began in 1951): in 1948 the electricity supply industry and the railways were nationalised and the National Health Service came into being. At local level, however, little had changed, and General Sir George Jeffreys' majority for the Conservatives, when he was returned as the Member of Parliament for East Hampshire in 1945, was hardly different from the majorities achieved by the same party in the constituency since the 1920s.

During the war years there had been a system of appointments to the Urban District Council; in 1946, however, the first democratic election of councillors for many years took place, and party politics played a bigger role as each seat on the Council was contested by several candidates. The Petersfield UDC continued to be responsible for the affairs of the town until 1974, when local government underwent radical changes, eliminating the old urban–rural distinction and replacing it with a Town Council and a District Council.

Other national political transformations took a little longer to implement fully: Petersfield County Secondary School (now the Petersfield School), created as a result of the Education Act of 1944, did not open its doors until 1958 and it was another seventeen years before primary school pupils (housed in the old Senior Council School in St Peter's Road) moved into their new premises, Herne Junior School, in Love Lane.

The major postwar estates in Petersfield began with the Cranford Road development (mid-1950s, some of the work being carried out by German prisoners of war), followed by the Durford Road estate (mid-1960s), and Herne Farm (begun in the 1960s and still expanding!). Regrettably for architectural conservationists, some of the more familiar buildings in the town were demolished at the same time: the Raglan development company from London proposed to alter the face of what, in some eyes, had become a 'ghost town' with many empty and neglected properties in the town centre. Fortunately for Petersfield and its inhabitants, only part of their comprehensive scheme was accepted. The year 1961 marked the turning point when the 'old Petersfield' began to disappear, and between 1961 and 1965 Raglan 'developed' Swan Court, the Girls' County High School, Clare Cross (Charles Dickins' surgery), Ganders (butchers), Bakers (butchers) and Childs (printers). David Money-Chappelle recalls the 1960s as a time when the pleasant, tired, sometimes depressing, war-bashed little country town of the fifties succumbed to a period of rapid change. Commercial growth was evident, cars appeared on The Square (a travesty, nevertheless!) and the character of the town visibly altered.

The cattle market in the 1950s. (Petersfield Museum)

Some may argue that the truly dilapidated buildings in the town were ripe for reconstruction, but since there were no preservation orders in those days it was impossible for anybody even to attempt to withstand the wholesale alteration of some towns and Petersfield suffered the fate of many such centres. It was partly because of the 'supermarket revolution' that in the 1960s some individual shops were forced to stop trading – a story one has heard with a certain regularity ever since, of course. As for Petersfield's transformation from a rural community with its own identity, towards a more commercially clinical and standardised late twentieth-century society, the year 1962, when the last cattle market was held in The Square, surely marks that passage quite clearly.

Progress in some form was, and is, however, inevitable. Farmers were certainly glad to rid themselves of the arduous physical tasks which were their lot: the arrival of combine harvesters, of milk tankers, of tractors and of more readily available and more efficient transportation methods were all introduced in the immediate postwar period. At Ellis's Sheet Mill, David and Clive Ellis joined their father in 1946 and continued the milling and haulage business until it was sold in 1970; here again, progress took the shape of a new fleet of large lorries (the originals having replaced the horse-drawn carts used in the early 1930s) which went direct to London docks to collect goods, instead of having them sent to Petersfield station for collection there. At the same time the Sheet Mill installed cubing and pelleting machines and produced complete animal food: this scientific-cum-technological advance saved farmers the task of concocting their own feeds from separate ingredients.

But what of the lessons learnt from the war, themselves indicative of incipient social change? What might be termed the 'moral effect' was a tangible consequence of the war. A frequent response to the question of how people coped under wartime conditions is a laconic 'we just had to get on with it', similar to the total equanimity displayed after a frightening experience: 'it's a wonder I wasn't shot'. The normally phlegmatic Briton was put to the test, but this engendered a tenacity of spirit which spread throughout the population. It also brought about changes in attitudes which no legislation could have achieved: a willingness to share a burden and join the war effort, a mixing of the social classes which was absent before the war, a sang-froid in the face of the horrors of war. Examples of such attitudes are demonstrated by the 85-year-old lady who volunteered to help Susie Fisher's team of kitchen staff at Adhurst St Mary with the washing up, the ready volunteers from all strata of Petersfield society at the Home from Home canteen, or the statement by Katie Pitt that 'we grew up very quickly' on recalling an incident at the Queen Alexandra Hospital when she had to give advice to the parents of a boy before they discovered that he had no eyelids and had lost part of his face. John Pownall has remarked that his wife's experience of social class mixing at the Itshide factory during the war was akin to what he saw during the period of national service after it.

By-products of wartime restrictions were the postwar concern for economy in everyday life (Mary Vincent's abstemiousness with sugar, Katie Pitt's hatred of the over-packaging of goods), and a tendency towards balanced living (in wartime people were forced to exercise more and to eat less). There was also a strong desire on the part of parents to prevent the next generation from experiencing the deprivation and horrors which war had brought. This, some would assert, led indirectly to the child-orientated revolution and changes in social attitudes of the decade after the war. Was child-pampering a product of this change? Did the political follow the social in this respect, and cause the election of the Labour government of 1945?

There was a slow, almost imperceptible, mutation taking place here in the whole of Britain; Petersfield, perhaps more than many towns, was lucky to experience evolutionary, rather than revolutionary, changes. What is certain is that, despite these changes, the town has indeed managed to preserve some of its old character. It has not been overrun by industrial development or architectural monstrosities, its demographic expansion has been rational and moderate, and, above all, there is vigilance by both public and private bodies for any threat to Petersfield's particular identity. For this Petersfielders should be thankful.

Major Events of the Second World War

1939: End of Spanish Civil War: Franco dictator (until 1975).
Germany annexes Czechoslovakia.
Italian troops invade Albania.
Molotov and von Ribbentrop sign Nazi-Soviet non-aggression pact.
Germany invades Poland (1 September).
Britain and France declare war on Germany.
Beginning of the 'phoney war'.
Battle of the River Plate.

1940: Italy and Japan side with Germany.
Germany invades Denmark, Norway, Belgium, Holland and Luxembourg.
Winston Churchill replaces Neville Chamberlain as Prime Minister.
Germany invades France.
Allied troops are evacuated from Dunkirk.
France surrenders; Vichy government under Marshal Pétain.
General de Gaulle leads Free French troops from London.
Battle of Britain (July–October); RAF defeats *Luftwaffe*.
Italy declares war on Britain and France and invades Greece.

1941: Australian and British troops capture Tobruk (Libya).
Italian and German troops invade Egypt.
Germany invades USSR.
Japanese attack on Pearl Harbor.
US declares war on Axis powers.
Malaya and Hong Kong captured by Japanese.

1942: Japanese capture Manila, Singapore, Indonesia, Philippines and Burma.
US sea victories stop Japanese advance.
Siege of Stalingrad.
Germans defeated at el Alamein, and retreat from North Africa.
Allies take Tripoli and Tunis.

1943: North Africa: all Axis resistance ends by May.
German troops surrender at Stalingrad.
Italian Fascist government of Mussolini surrenders.
US begins to recapture Japanese-held islands.

1944: Allies defeat remaining Fascist forces in Italy.
Allies land in Normandy (D-Day 6 June).
German forces retreat.
Allies liberate Paris and Brussels.
V1 bombs and V2 rockets land on London.
Japanese Navy defeated by US Navy in the Pacific.

1945: Soviet troops march into Poland and capture Warsaw.
Yalta conference to discuss postwar settlements.
Allied troops cross into Germany.
Dresden heavily bombed.
US President Roosevelt dies; Truman succeeds him.
Mussolini assassinated.
Soviet Army reaches Berlin.
Hitler commits suicide.
Germany surrenders (7 May).
VE Day (8 May).
US drops atomic bombs on Hiroshima and Nagasaki: Japan surrenders.
VJ Day (15 August).

Biographies

Karin ANTONINI (née BARNSLEY) (b. 1927)
Born near Petersfield and educated locally from 1930 to 1943. Did unpaid work on props for the London Ballet Company, then studied theatrical design in London from 1943 to 1947. After various unpaid jobs and a secretarial course moved to Paris. Worked in UNESCO from 1951 to 1966. Married Giacomo Antonini in 1961, had a son in 1963, then moved to the Petersfield area in 1967. Taught French at a local prep school for ten years, then became Secretary to the Edward Barnsley Educational Trust and Furniture Workshop.

Wilson ATKINSON (b. 1927)
Born at Lower Farm, East Meon. Educated at East Meon School, then at Churcher's Prep and College from 1933 to 1943. Left school and returned to the farm, first working with his father, eventually managing 1,200 acres. Retired in 1995. Served on many farming clubs and committees and the East Meon parish and village hall councils. His son George is now running the estate.

April AUSTIN (née WOODFIELD) (b. 1929)
Born in Carshalton, Surrey. Educated in Surrey and Sussex; the family moved to Sheet in 1939 and she attended Petersfield County High School during the war years. In 1946 she and her mother Muriel, who had worked for Dick Wilkins in the Billeting Office during the war, emigrated to Alberta, Canada, where they literally pioneered. She began nursing training in 1954, qualified in 1957, the year of her marriage, and subsequently followed careers in nursing and secretarial work. She has three sons and two grandsons and now lives near Vancouver. She recently enjoyed a return visit to Sheet and Petersfield.

Ted BAIGENT (b. 1926)
Born in Haslemere. After the death of his father in 1932 the family moved to Sheet where his mother had spent her childhood. Apart from a few years in the RAF, when he served for a short time in Burma, he has lived in the Petersfield area and until retirement was a Legal Executive with a local firm of solicitors. He has been a Voluntary Warden with English Nature (formerly the Nature Conservancy Council) for over forty years.

Victoria BALL (née WARDLE) (b. 1940)
Born in Singapore, the second daughter of Victor and Betty Wardle. Arrived in Petersfield in 1945, living with her maternal grandmother, F. Helen Luker, at 22 High Street, the Luker home from 1875 to 1950. Attended Miss Williams's Kindergarten, then Seager House (until recently Moreton House), followed by boarding school and college. Taught in schools in London, Surrey and Herefordshire before returning to Petersfield in 1994.

George BARNES (b. 1917)
Born at Clipsham in Rutland and educated at Stamford School and St John's College, Cambridge. He was appointed to the staff of Churcher's College in 1939 to teach mathematics. After war service in the Royal Corps of Signals (1940–6), he returned to Churcher's and retired in 1982.

Captain Michael BARROW (b. 1932)

Captain Barrow was born in Surrey, but on the outbreak of war in 1939 and his father's recall to the Royal Navy the family moved to the Petersfield area, living successively in Heath Road, at Woolbeding, at Steep Farm and, towards the end of the war, in Liss. They did not return to Surrey after the war, preferring the Hampshire countryside. Michael Barrow has lived at Shear Hill since 1973, after a career in the Royal Navy and in the City.

Roy BARROW (b. 1935)

Comes from an old Buriton family dating back over two centuries. After the war he was one of the first pupils of the newly named Petersfield Secondary Modern School in St Peter's Road. He married at eighteen, then moved to Alton and worked in the aircraft engineering industry. His hobbies included playing in a repertory company. He finished his career in the antique dealing business. Celebrates his golden wedding anniversary in 2004.

John BRIDLE (b. 1907)

Born and brought up in Petersfield. His earliest memory is seeing the local fire engine being drawn by horses on the way to a fire. Attended the Infants School in Hylton Road in 1911 and eventually Churcher's College in 1921. He remembers well the visit of Princess Beatrice to the school in 1922. On leaving Churcher's his first employment was with Britnell and Crawter Ltd, Automobile Engineers, College Street. In 1931 he joined an assurance company as a member of the 'field staff'. In 1935 he was offered a post in the Horsham District, and remained there until his retirement in 1967. Both he and his wife thought of Petersfield as their home and returned to the town soon afterwards.

June BROOKS (née GANDER) (b. 1928)

Grandfather Henry Gander started the family butcher's business in the High Street in the 1880s. June lived with her grandmother in Ramshill during the war years and attended Portsmouth High School (at Adhurst St Mary) before going to boarding school. During the war she was involved in the many concerts and fund-raising events organised by her mother (Hilda Goode), whose first husband, Reg, had died in 1930. In 1945 she entered the family business until her marriage in 1949 to Donald Brooks, who later became Headmaster of Churcher's College.

Joan BULLEN (née CARPENTER) (b. 1908)

The second daughter and one of the eight children of Mr and Mrs Frank Carpenter. Attended the church school in Hylton Road and lived most of her childhood at the other end of that road. After being a pupil at the Petersfield Girls' Secondary School in the High Street she studied at the Portsmouth School of Art. Became a governess at The Grange in 1927, then taught in various schools, finally at Churcher's Prep School in the 1930s. She married Norman in 1937, they moved to Surrey and had three children. After retirement they moved to Cornwall, where she still lives, indulging in her favourite hobby of painting.

Richard BURLEY (b. 1932)

The first baby to be born in the then new maternity wing of the old Petersfield Hospital, he spent his early life in the family home in Bell Hill. Attended Miss Williams's Kindergarten at Winton House, then Churcher's Prep School. Went to boarding school in 1942 owing to his father's war service. After national service he returned in 1952 and became articled in the family firm of solicitors Burley & Geach. Joined the local Territorial Army for five years. Rejoined the family firm in 1957 and finally retired as senior partner in 1990. His family lived for many years in East Meon where he became involved in local affairs, both there and also in Petersfield.

Peggy CARPENTER (née CROOKS) (b. 1923)
Born in north-west London and moved to Battersea in 1935, attending Battersea Central School until 1939 (immediately before they evacuated to Petersfield, as she discovered by chance later). Left London and met her husband in 1940. They moved to his home village of Liss in 1949, where she still lives. Worked briefly at F.W. Childs, the printers, after the war, finally spending nearly twenty years in the Civil Service, before retiring in 1983.

Margaret CHILDS (b. 1925)
Was at school in Sheet and Petersfield before leaving for Hereford at the age of fourteen to stay briefly with an uncle. Returned to Petersfield at the outbreak of war and worked for a year at Bassetts, the ironmongers. Then she found employment at the post office, first as a telephonist, then as an instructor in Aldershot and Guildford training schools and finally back to Petersfield where she was put in charge of the telephone exchange. She finished her forty-two-year career in telecommunications as a BT service rep until her retirement owing to ill health in 1983.

Norma COLLINS (née GUY) (b. 1928)
Born in Sheet, and brought up at Lower Adhurst Farm, where her father was the dairyman. Educated at Sheet and Petersfield Council Schools. Worked in Edward Privett's shop in the High Street, then Rowland, Son and Vincent. Married Ronald, a Petersfield man born and bred, in 1952. Member of Sheet Choir, the Church Youth Club and the Sheet Troupers. Finally worked with the Hampshire Library Service and Social Services. Since retirement has been helping at Herne Junior School.

George COOK (b. 1923)
Born in Portsmouth and educated at Portsmouth Grammar School. He moved to Petersfield in 1942 after his home in Old Portsmouth was destroyed in the January blitz of 1941. During the Second World War he joined the Fleet Air Arm and served in the Pacific. After the war he embarked on a career in horticulture and trained at Hilliers Nurseries in Winchester before going into business himself. He ran his own nursery in Petersfield from 1950 to 1970 and has now lived in the town for over sixty years.

Dorothy COOMBES (née POINTER) (b. 1914)
Was educated and worked in Portsmouth until her marriage in 1937. Her husband Ian's grandparents had brought him up in Petersfield and so, to avoid the bombing in Portsmouth where Ian had enlisted in the Royal Marines, the couple eventually decided to settle in Sheet with their two young children. Ian was a survivor of the HMS *Royal Oak* sinking in October 1939, but lost his life two years later on HMS *Hereward* off Crete, only months after seeing his wife and children for the last time shortly after Christmas 1940. Dorothy began work in the Civil Service in 1943, becoming officer in charge of the Food Office for East Hampshire until rationing ended. She then joined the staff of the Employment Exchange until her retirement in 1975.

Lou CROSSWELL (b. 1931)
Born in Folkestone. The family moved to Wandsworth, London, in 1935, where Lou attended junior school. He then gained a scholarship to Emanuel School and so arrived in Petersfield in September 1942 and stayed until 1944. After a national service commission in the RAF he was employed as a company secretary for a building contractor. He was also a keen rugby and cricket player for Old Emanuel teams. He married in 1954, has two children and three grandchildren, and is living in Wandsworth again.

Jenny DANDRIDGE (née BURLEY) (b. 1935)
Born in Petersfield and one of the third generation of Burleys to live in the town. Apart from a period in the war when her father was stationed in the Midlands and for ten years after leaving school she has been here all her life. She remembers the workhouse bomb as she was at school only 200 yards away. Married in 1955 and joined the Bedales staff in 1969 as a home economics teacher. Has also taught textiles and design. Retired and still very busy.

Philip EADES (b. 1935)
Born in Winchester, his family settled first in Cranford Road, then moved to Buriton. Spent his wartime years at Buriton Primary School, then went to Churcher's College. At the age of sixteen he was employed in a local architect's office where, apart from two years' national service in the RAF, he remained until he set up his own architectural practice in 1976. Married with two daughters and now retired and living in Buriton.

Clive ELLIS (b. 1920)
Born at Sheet Mill House. Attended Miss Williams's Kindergarten in Petersfield, then Sheet School and finally Churcher's College, from 1930 until 1937. He was articled to the engineer and surveyor of Petersfield Urban District Council and at the same time studied for an External Degree in Civil Engineering at London University. Being found medically unfit to serve in the Armed Forces, he joined a firm of quantity surveyors employed by the Admiralty Engineering Service based in Portsmouth dockyard. After the war he rejoined the UDC to assist in the development of the Cranford Road housing scheme. When the infrastructure to this project was completed he joined the family firm of J. Ellis & Sons and remained there until the firm was acquired by Unilever in 1970.

Miriam ELLIS (née LAISHLEY) (b. 1939)
Born in Portsmouth, she was first evacuated to Lyme Regis, and then brought up in a children's home in London where she stayed until her late teens. She spent many holidays with her grandparents, the Daughtrys, in Petersfield, finally living with them for a while. She began a career in nursery nursing and remained a nurse for forty years, including a period at Le Court. Now retired and living in the same street in Petersfield where her grandparents used to live.

Susie FISHER (née KERTLAND) (b. 1912)
Born in Portsmouth, educated at the Francis Avenue School, then the Municipal College where she gained a scholarship to enable her to train for a Domestic Science Diploma. Worked in many spheres, latterly at Adhurst St Mary during the war, with the girls evacuated from Portsmouth High School. Since her retirement in Petersfield she has been doing voluntary work.

Amy FREEMAN (b. 1908)
Born at Wenham Holt Lodge in Rake and educated at Rake School and Petersfield High School. She trained to be a teacher at Salisbury Training College (1926–8) and taught in East Sussex and Woking during the war years. Weekends were spent with her parents at Farther Common, and she particularly remembers the Lancaster bombers heading for the Continent coming over at tree-top height. She joined Petersfield Infants School in 1950 and retired as Deputy Headmistress in 1969. She still enjoys being greeted by her former pupils.

John FREEMAN (b. 1921)
Born and educated in Petersfield. Left school in 1935 and went into the family hairdressing business. Joined the RAF in 1941. After the war went back to the family business until his retirement in 1985.

Dennis GEEN (b. 1924)
Spent his childhood in London until his school (Emanuel) was evacuated to Petersfield on the outbreak of war in September 1939. With the security offered by a very comfortable billet, over the following three years he formed an enduring attachment to the town and its environs. On retiring from government service in 1984 he returned to Petersfield where he now lives, contentedly pursuing his many interests.

Shirley GEORGE (née **ALDRED**) (b. 1926)
Born in Osborne Road, Petersfield, and attended the Council School in St Peter's Road. At the age of nine she moved with her family to Dunhill Cottage on the Bedales estate at Steep. During the war they used the underground shelter provided by Bedales School during the night-time raids. At the age of fourteen she left school and began work for Petersfield Rural Council in the billeting department. Shortly after her marriage at the age of twenty-three she stopped work. She and her husband had two children and were married for forty-six years.

Josephine GILLMORE (b. 1928)
Born in Portsmouth, but evacuated to West Mark Camp when it opened in 1939 and remained there for nearly five years, the longest serving pupil at the school. After the war she worked in the drapery business, then in aircraft manufacturing in Portsmouth. She retired in 1989. Has visited Australia, having been inspired to do so by her geography teacher at West Mark Camp.

Nick HALL (b. 1941)
After the family had been bombed out of two houses in Southsea and machine-gunned out of another, his parents moved first to Hitchin, Herts, then to Petersfield, where they spent the duration of the war in a tack room in the grounds of Fenns, in Reservoir Lane. Back in Portsmouth at the end of the war Nick went to St John's College, then entered the Bermuda Police Service from 1962 to 1969. Returned to Portsmouth and went into property management until 1987, also serving as a Captain in the Territorial Army. He then started Sabre Sales in Southsea, a shop specialising in military uniforms and paraphernalia, his life-long passion.

Ron HATTON (b. 1929)
Born and raised in Portsmouth, with the exception of two years at West Mark Camp School (1940–2) as an evacuee. On leaving West Mark returned to Portsmouth where he delivered newspapers every day, often during fierce air raids. At age sixteen apprenticed as a plumber and gas fitter after serving three years at Portsmouth Building School. At twenty-one called up for national service and served with the RAF, then with BAFO in Germany as an airframe mechanic. In 1954 returned to civilian life as a plumber and heating engineer. Now retired in Portchester.

Jennifer HAYNE (née **WOOODHOUSE**) (b. 1931)
Born in Southsea, lived in Petersfield from 1937 to 1944. Became a naval wife, as well as a naval daughter, thus necessitating several moves. Settled in Petersfield again after she was widowed in 1998.

David JEFFERY (b. 1938)
Born, brought up and educated in London. Spent a certain proportion of the war years either wrapped in a red dressing gown in a cellar with his mother in the next-door neighbours' house, or crouching in a Morrison shelter in the back room at home. After university he trained and worked as a modern languages teacher. When he was appointed to Bedales staff in 1983 the family left London for good, settled in the Petersfield area and fell in love with it. Now semi-retired, he was inspired to write this book after meeting some elderly Petersfield residents on a minibus he drives for Age Concern.

Peter LYNE (b. 1927)
Joined Emanuel in 1936 and came to Petersfield from 1939 to 1945. Was in charge of hiring the lorries to take the school equipment back to Wandsworth. Also ran the school National Savings group. Joined a firm of accountants in the City of London and spent the whole of his working life with various audit firms in the City. Thirteen years ago suggested to his wife that they should leave Greater London and move to Petersfield. She fell in love with the town and the surrounding area and they have been here ever since.

Peter MACKARNESS (b. 1919)
Born in Scarborough but brought up in Worcestershire. Educated at Bradfield College, then moved to Petersfield at the age of nineteen. His war service was spent in the Royal Engineers and Royal Artillery from 1939 until 1946, during which time he was in the UK and NW Europe, including being in the D-Day action in Normandy. Afterwards he entered the Petersfield family firm of solicitors started by his great uncle in the 1890s, from which he retired in 1983.

Dr David MARTIN (b. 1936)
Born, brought up and educated in Petersfield. He spent much of the war in part-time schooling in very large classes and sheltering under stairs during air raids. He trained in London as a doctor, qualifying in 1961. Having worked in various hospitals in Portsmouth, Jersey and Bournemouth, he spent thirty years as a general practitioner in Waterlooville, retiring in 1996. He is now involved in many charitable works and is a governor of four independent schools.

Peter MATTINGLEY (b. 1923)
Born in Witley, Surrey, and moved to Petersfield with his parents in the early 1930s. Educated at Churcher's College, followed by a brief period as a junior clerk with the local branch of Barclays Bank, before being able to volunteer for the RAF in 1941. Served in Burma. Spent the majority of his working life as a life underwriter, from which he retired eighteen years ago. Now lives in Petersfield.

Roy MAXWELL (b. 1926)
Born in Wandsworth and educated at local elementary school. Won a scholarship to Emanuel School in 1937, and evacuated to Petersfield in 1939. Gained a First in Engineering at London University in 1947, then worked as a Scientific Officer in armaments during his national service. In 1959 moved to Cornwall to work on aircraft-launched torpedoes, then to the Royal Aircraft Estabishment at Farnborough where he became an international specialist in metal fatigue. Moved to Petersfield in 1983 and retired in 1986 as the RAE Head of Structural Airworthiness Division. Keen on cricket, golf and amateur dramatics while in Petersfield. He now lives on the Isle of Wight.

David MONEY-CHAPPELLE (b. 1933)
Born in Hong Kong and educated at Dean Close School, Cheltenham. He served as an Aircrew Officer in the RAF and afterwards worked in the film, newspaper and travel industries. In 1973 he formed DMC Associates, his own management and marketing consultancy with his wife June, while continuing to write freelance. He moved to Petersfield in 1986 and then to Steep Marsh, where he now lives in semi-retirement. He swims regularly at the Petersfield open-air pool and he and his wife are keen supporters of the Petersfield Youth Theatre.

Mary MONEY-CHAPPELLE (b. 1935)
Born in Portsmouth, educated at Seager House and Upper Chine School, Isle of Wight. Studied singing at the Guildhall School of Music and Drama. Sang professionally in England and Ireland, entertained troops in Northern Ireland for Combined Services, has played in musicals, and performed on radio and television. Led the singing in Petersfield market square at reception and service on VE Day 1945.

Geoffrey PADDOCK (b. 1931)
Born, brought up and educated in Petersfield. His wartime memories are of warm summers and cold winters; the war seemed, at times, very distant. Called up for national service (1950–2). On return he entered local government where he remained until his retirement in 1993.

Steve PIBWORTH (b. 1929)
Born in Southsea, moved to Stroud in 1934. Attended Churcher's Prep under Mr Le Grice, then Churcher's College. The family had moved to Oakfield (in Love Lane) just before the workhouse bomb fell. Became Chairman of Petersfield Angling Club at the age of thirteen. Did his national service in the Royal Engineers and was posted first to Egypt, then to Kenya. Returning home, he started working for Joe Smith at The Forge (ostensibly for six weeks) and is still there after fifty-four years.

Kathleen PITT (b. 1924)
Born in Hill Brow, Liss, and moved to Petersfield in 1939. Educated at Winton House Prep and Petersfield High School. Trained as a Red Cross nurse and worked at Queen Alexandra hospital from D-Day onwards. Was Leonard Cheshire's first helper in 1950. Also trained in Paris and Zurich in the 1960s and travelled widely with work. Returned to Petersfield in 1985 and worked with Sue Ryder. Elected Town Councillor 1991–2003, and Town Mayor 1998–9.

Brigadier John POWNALL (b. 1929)
Lived in London until the outbreak of war when the family moved to live with grandmother at Broadlands, Sheet, which was sold in 1946. Educated at Rugby and RMA Sandhurst. Commissioned into 16th/5th Lancers and served in command and staff appointments in Egypt, North Africa, BAOR, Hong Kong and Cyprus. Retired 1984. Deputy Chairman of the Police Complaints Authority 1985–94. Chairman of Petersfield Decorative and Fine Arts Society 1997–2001. Home has been in Milland since 1964.

Mary RAY (née PEARSON) (b. 1926)
Born in Bristol in the same week that her father Guy bought Gammon and Smith's in Petersfield, to which the family then moved. After Winton House and Petersfield County

High School, she joined Portsmouth High School in 1942 (at Adhurst St Mary). After studying geography and anthropology at university she took a teaching diploma. Married Alan in 1949; soon afterwards her father died and Alan took over the family business in Petersfield, while she taught for two years at the Girls' High School. They bought Goodyers in 1957, where their five children were brought up. Alan became Mayor of Petersfield, and Mary has been actively involved with the Historical Society, the Guides, the Physic Garden, the Choral Society and the museum. Alan died in 1992.

Charles SAMMONDS (b. 1926)

Born and bred in the slums of Battersea, educated at Battersea Central School for Boys and, after evacuation to Empshott at the outbreak of war, transferred to Emanuel School in Petersfield. Served in Military Intelligence from 1944 to 1946, demobbed as lieutenant RA in 1948. Became an authority on the use of carbon in high temperature refractories. Finally retired as Head of Postgraduate Studies from Wolverhampton Business School.

David SCURFIELD (b. 1939)

Moved to Petersfield in 1941 when he experienced, not without tears, a simulated *blitzkrieg* on the nearby Town Hall (from his pram). He has spent much of his life moving from house to house around Petersfield Heath, when not involved in typography, printing, engraving glass, and occasionally extracting money from the public for the Save the Children Fund by flogging books.

John STACE (b. 1919)

Born the son of a yeoman farmer in East Sussex and educated in local schools. Was a sapper in the war, serving in the UK, India and Burma. Became a quantity surveyor from 1946 until his retirement. Regrettably, without the untimely intervention of tuberculosis, he might have become a professional singer. Married to Mary Barnes.

Mary STACE (née BARNES) (b. 1918)

Born in Southsea and educated in Portsmouth. She qualified as a teacher in 1939, but was evacuated to Salisbury at the beginning of the war. She later moved to East Meon, married John in 1946, then moved to Bedhampton in 1948. She taught in local schools and became a headteacher in 1975. She retired in 1978.

Graeme TRIGGS (b. 1939)

Born in a bedroom above his father's outfitting shop in Lavant Street, where he was to work for forty-three years. On leaving Sheet Primary School went to Petersfield Secondary School. During his national service he was in the Army Catering Corps ('Andy Capp's Commandos') at Aldershot. Since his retirement in 1997 he has lived in Cowplain.

Sheila TRUEMAN (née HADEN) (b. 1926)

Born in Wiltshire, she and her older sister boarded at Bedales from 1937 and were joined there by their two younger sisters at the beginning of the war. Went to Oxford University after the war and married Reginald Trueman in 1949. Between 1949 and 1972 they lived in New York, Bolton, Hong Kong, London and Newcastle. In 1966 they bought a cottage in Sheet for holiday use. Both she and her husband retired from teaching in 1982 and settled in Sheet where they stayed until 1996, apart from two years spent in Lesotho. They moved to Church Path, next to the Flora Twort Gallery, in 1996.

Mary VINCENT (b. 1936)
Born in old Petersfield Hospital. Went to school in Sheet, then Petersfield Secondary School (in St Peter's Road) and Brightside in Havant. After a brief sojourn in Alverstoke (NCHO) joined the family business of Rowland, Son and Vincent as a temp in accounts and sales. Took over the running of the Funeral Services department in the 1980s after passing the Diploma exam. Elected to Town Council 1996 and became Mayor of Petersfield in 2002.

Victor WALKER (b. 1924)
Born locally and educated at the local Council School and at Churcher's College until 1941. Served as a dispatch rider with the National Fire Service in Petersfield until 1943 before joining the Royal Warwickshire Regiment. Later commissioned in the Devonshire Regiment and served in the 6th Airborne Division, taking part in the D-Day landings in Normandy in 1944. After being invalided out of the Army he returned to Petersfield and began training as a quantity surveyor in 1948 at the Northern Polytechnic, London. Married Madeleine in 1948 at the Wesleyan church, Station Road, and has two sons. Started in practice as a quantity surveyor in 1948, retiring in 1989; he is still engaged in consultancy work. He has resided in Petersfield for over seventy years.

Madeleine WALKER (née JONES) (b. 1926)
Born in Waterlooville, but moved to Portsmouth and joined Portsmouth High School in 1937. Evacuated first to Hinton Ampner, then to Adhurst St Mary in 1941. When her parents moved to Petersfield she became a day girl until July 1944. Studied at King's College School of Physiotherapy. Occasionally assisted her parents in the administration of Bell Hill Manufacturing Company. Returned to live in Petersfield, where she and Victor were married in 1948.

A.J. 'Dick' WILKINS (b. 1913)
Born in Southsea, he remembers seeing a zeppelin caught in searchlights over London in the First World War. He was educated at King's College School, Wimbledon, then went into business. He married in 1938, one year before coming to Petersfield to work for the Urban District Council and the then Ministry of Health in connection with the Government Evacuation Scheme. He became the Chief Billeting Officer and was also vice-controller of the ARP control centre at the Town Hall. After the war he pursued his hobby of flying for twenty-five years after obtaining his private pilot's licence. Sadly, he lost his wife after forty years of marriage. He now lives in Devon with his second wife Edna.

Peter WINSCOM (b. 1921)
Born at Wardley Farm in Milland, where his father farmed. In 1933 the family moved to Red House, Stroud, to farm Stroud Farm on the retirement of his maternal grandparents. He went straight from school to work on the farm; although he wanted to join up in the early days of the war he was in a reserved occupation and so stayed in Stroud. In 1947 he married a farmer's daughter, Anne Mason, from Bedhampton. Over the years he has acquired neighbouring land and he now farms, with his manager, nearly 1,000 acres, from Stroud to Butser via Weston.

Bibliography

BOOKS

BONIFACE, R.S., *Petersfield Town brochure* (Official Guide), 1938
Brandreth, G. and Henry, S., *Bedales School and its Founder*, 1967
Brown, M., *Evacuees*, Sutton Publishing, 2000
Churcherian, The, Vol. V (1936–9) & Vol. VI (1940–6)
Darwin, B., *War on the Line*, Middleton Press, 1946
Farnham, D. and Dine, D., *Petersfield Seen and Remembered*, Hampshire County Library, 1982
Giles, L.C., *Liphook, Bramshott and the Canadians*, Blackwell Press, Liphook 1986
Godfrey, A., *Petersfield 1908*, Old Ordnance Survey Maps, Hampshire Sheet 52.16, 1908
History Encyclopedia, Kingfisher, 1992
Hammerton, Sir J., *The War Illustrated*, Vol. 1, Amalgamated Press, 1940
Hampshire Federation of Women's Institutes, *Hampshire within Living Memory*, Countryside Books, 1994
Leighton, T., *West Mark Camp School, 1940–1945*, An Anniversary Remembrance, (pamphlet), 1985
Levy, Arnold, *This I Recall (1939–1945)*, St Catherine's Press, 1945
Life on the Home Front, The Reader's Digest, 1993
Longmate, N., *How we lived then*, Pimlico, 1971
Marjoribanks, R., *Emanuel at Wandsworth, 1883–1983*, Ludo Press, 1983
Minty, E. Arden, *Some Account of the History of Petersfield*, John Lane, The Bodley Head, 1923
Mitchell, V. and Smith, K., *Branch Lines around Midhurst*, Middleton Press, 1987
Munro-Faure, A., *Flora Twort, A Petersfield Artist*, Hampshire Papers, 1995
Old Emanuel Association, *Newsletters*, Summer 1999, February 2001
Porter, V., *Yesterday's Countryside*, David and Charles, 2000
Rand, H., *A Book of Petersfield*, illus. by Reg Gammon, A.W. Childs, Petersfield, 1927
Residents of The Hartings and Nyewood, *Wartime Memories 1939–1945*, One Tree Books, 1995
Stamp, W., *'Doctor Himself', an Unorthodox Biography of Harry Roberts*, Hamish Hamilton, 1949
Street, S., *Petersfield: A Pictorial Past*, Ensign Publications, 1989
Wardle, Betty, *Family Journal – the War Years*, Southern Press, 1984
Williams, The Revd J., *The History of Petersfield*, in *Petersfield, A Pictorial Past*, 1857

Government Documents

Brophy, J., *A Home Guard Handbook* (11th edn), Wyman & Sons, 1943
Evelyn Thomas, S., *ARP, A Practical Guide for the Householder and Air-Raid Warden*, Simkin Marshall Ltd
Fire Guards Handbook, The (Air Raid Precautions Handbook No. 14), HMSO, 1942
National Service, HMSO, 1939
Protection of your Home Against Raids, The, Home Office, HMSO, 1938

Petersfield Area Historical Society Bulletins

Bennetts, Mrs, *Memories of Old Petersfield*, (Sheet School), Autumn 1977
Burnham, W., *I.T.S. Rubber Ltd*, Spring 1997
Coupland, S., *Petersfield High School for Girls*, Spring 1991
Fisher, S., *Portsmouth High School Evacuees at Sheet*, Spring 1986
Gard, J., *South East Farmers Ltd*, Autumn 1985
——, *V.E. Day Remembered*, Spring 1995
Henstock, I. (arr. by Mary Ray), *Bordean House War Work*, Spring 1981

Lunt, M., *Some Personal Reminiscences*, Spring 1983

——, *The Second World War – Some Personal Reminiscences*, Spring 1994

May, E., *Pride of the Petersfield Firefighters*, Spring 1995

Miller, Mr, (arr. by Marjorie Lunt), *Memories of Old Petersfield (Heath House)*, Spring 1981

Piggott, M., *Hop-picking*, Spring 1984

Prichard, J., *A Profile of Monty & Dorothy Beagley: A Story of Country Folk*, Spring 1994

——, *Memories of V.E. Day*, Spring 1995

——, *Local Associations with the Free French and Free Dutch Navies during World War Two*, Autumn 1995

Ray, M., HMS *Suthers*, Spring 1979

——, *To War with a Needle and Thread*, Spring 1979

——, *Petersfield Canteens (1939–46)*, Spring 1983

——, *The Royal Observer Corps*, Spring 1994

——, *Wartime Schooling and D-Day*, Spring 1994

Some Memories of Hilda Barnes, A Spy at Sheet (arr. by Marjorie Lunt), Autumn 1997

Standfield, F.G., *Petersfield Workhouse Bombing*, Autumn 1985

Walker, J., *Petersfield Workhouse*, Autumn 1996

Wardle, B., *Luker's Brewery*, Spring 1984

White, P. (arr. by Mary Ray), *Camouflage Netting Manufacture*, Spring 1981

Sheet News Articles

Cawsey, A., *Another view of Emanuel School in Petersfield*, March 2001

Clarke, G., *Village Profiles (no. 9): Norma Collins*, September 1997

——, *Village Profiles (no. 11): John Lovell*, September, 1998

——, *Village Profiles (no.15): The Passingham Family (Part 1)*, September 2000

——, *Village Profiles (no. 16): The Passingham Family (Part 2)*, March 2001

——, *Village Profiles (no. 18): Margaret Childs*, March 2002

Clarke, V., *Their Name Liveth for Evermore*, September 1995

——, *Emanuel School in Petersfield (1–8)*, March 1997–March 2001

Fisher, Mrs S., *The Pleasures of Rural Evacuation*, Interview with Vaughan Clarke, March 1995

Gibson, S. and O., *Village Profiles (no. 2)*, Interview with Gillian Clarke, March 1994

Pibworth, S., *Village Profiles (no. 5)*, Interview with Gillian Clarke, September 1995

Ray, M., *West Mark Camp: Memories of Mrs Vera Johnson 1941–1946*, September 2000

Stokes, G., *Recollections of Wartime in Sheet*, September 1995

Petersfield Area Historical Society (PAHS) Documents

Gard, J. et al., *High Street, Petersfield* (Petersfield Monograph, no. 2), 1984

Inns of Petersfield, The (Petersfield Papers, no. 3), PAHS, 1977

Leaton, E. et al., *A History of Christianity in Petersfield* (Petersfield Monograph, no.4), 2001

Lunt, M. and Ray M., *Petersfield Music Makers* (Petersfield Monograph, no. 3), 1986

Petersfield Perambulation, A (Petersfield Papers, no. 9), PAHS, 1996

Petersfield Place Names (Petersfield Papers, no. 1, 3rd. Edition), PAHS, 2000

Petersfield Society Newsletter

Scurfield, D., *To School and Back: 1940s Petersfield*, Spring 1991

Newspaper

Hants and Sussex News, 1938–46

Index